HOUGHTON MIFFLIN HARCOURT

Write-In Reader

Grade 6

Printed in the U.S.A.

ISBN   978-0-547-90903-5

15 16 17   0877   21 20 19 18 17 16 15

4500529366   A B C D E F G

HOUGHTON MIFFLIN HARCOURT

School Publishers

Be a Reading Detective!

Welcome to your *Write-In Reader*! With this book, you will be a **Reading Detective**. You will look for clues in stories and in nonfiction selections. The clues will help you

- ▶ **enjoy stories,**

- ▶ **understand nonfiction,**

- ▶ **answer questions, and**

- ▶ **be a great reader!**

A Reading Detective can solve the mystery of any reading selection. No selection is too hard! A Reading Detective **asks questions**. A Reading Detective **reads carefully**.

Asking questions and reading carefully will help you **find clues**. Then, you will

- ▶ **stop,**

- ▶ **think, and**

- ▶ **write!**

Let's try it! Follow the trail . . .

In the box is the beginning of a story. Read carefully. Ask yourself questions:

▶ **Who is the story about?**

▶ **Where and when does the story take place?**

▶ **What is happening?**

Look for clues to answer your questions.

> Logan was enjoying his bike ride. He felt the warm sun on his face. He smelled the beach nearby. He heard his dad humming on the bike in front of him. So far, Logan was having a great birthday.
>
> Suddenly, Logan screeched to a stop.
>
> "Dad!" he called out. "Look at that!"

Stop   Think   Write

Where and when does the story take place? How do you know?

_____

_____

Did you read carefully? Did you look for clues? Did the clues help you answer the questions? If they did, you are already a **Reading Detective**!

Contents

✓ **TARGET VOCABULARY**

disclose
muted
pressuring
revisions
wry

A Poetry Contest

1 My school was having a poetry contest. The best poem in each class would be published in our school newspaper. Students weren't required to submit a poem, but my friend Emil was **pressuring** me to write one. He knew that I loved poetry.

Tell about a time when someone was <u>pressuring</u> you to do better work in school or in sports.

_____

_____

_____

2 One rule was that the author of each poem must not **disclose** his or her identity until after the voting. Everyone in the class would get a vote. Our principal wanted to make sure that students voted on the poems without being influenced by who wrote them.

Write a synonym of <u>disclose</u>.

_____

2

3 I wrote about a rainstorm that had flooded our basement and ruined some family photographs. Parts of the poem were funny. My parents told me that I had a **wry** sense of humor to be able to joke about something so serious.

Describe another situation where you could make a <u>wry</u> joke.

_____

_____

_____

4 I worked hard on my poem and made several **revisions**. I changed some of the rhymes and punctuation until my poem sounded just right.

What kinds of <u>revisions</u> might you make to an essay about your favorite author?

_____

_____

_____

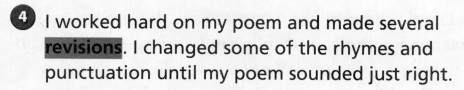

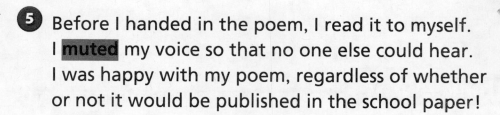

5 Before I handed in the poem, I read it to myself. I **muted** my voice so that no one else could hear. I was happy with my poem, regardless of whether or not it would be published in the school paper!

Tell about a time when you <u>muted</u> your voice. Why did you speak quietly?

_____

_____

Song for the Whales

by Mia Lewis

Every year, the whales stopped in our cove during their six-thousand-mile trip south from the Bering Sea. They always seemed to be traveling slowly, as if they had all the time in the world. They swam right into the cove next to our town and stayed there for days. You could see them splashing their tails and looking at everyone on the beach.

People came from far away to see those huge and amazing creatures. Binoculars in hand, spectators stood on the sand and gazed out at the whales. The whales seemed to like the attention. They would dive and spout water almost as if they were performing for us. I couldn't imagine feeling so comfortable with all those people watching me. Just the idea of performing made me freeze up like a block of ice.

Stop Think Write

UNDERSTANDING CHARACTERS

What do the whales seem to be able to do that the narrator cannot?

_____

_____

_____

4

I loved spending time at the cove, but I usually went when no one else was around. You see, the beach was a great spot to write my songs. I sat on the rocks with my notebook and wrote down tunes and lyrics. I don't think I could have written a word if I thought someone might be looking over my shoulder. However, sitting by myself next to the sea, I sometimes wrote for hours. No one was **pressuring** me to work faster. I could make as many **revisions** as I wanted before a song was finished.

After I wrote the songs, I tried singing them. I felt too shy to sing in front of people, but the whales were a great audience! They swam and jumped in the cove while I sang. They seemed to like my songs, and I knew they would never **disclose** my secret. I hadn't told my family or friends about my songs. I wasn't ready to share my music yet. I wasn't sure I'd ever be ready.

Stop Think Write

VOCABULARY

What may the narrator never <u>disclose</u> to his family and friends?

_____

_____

_____

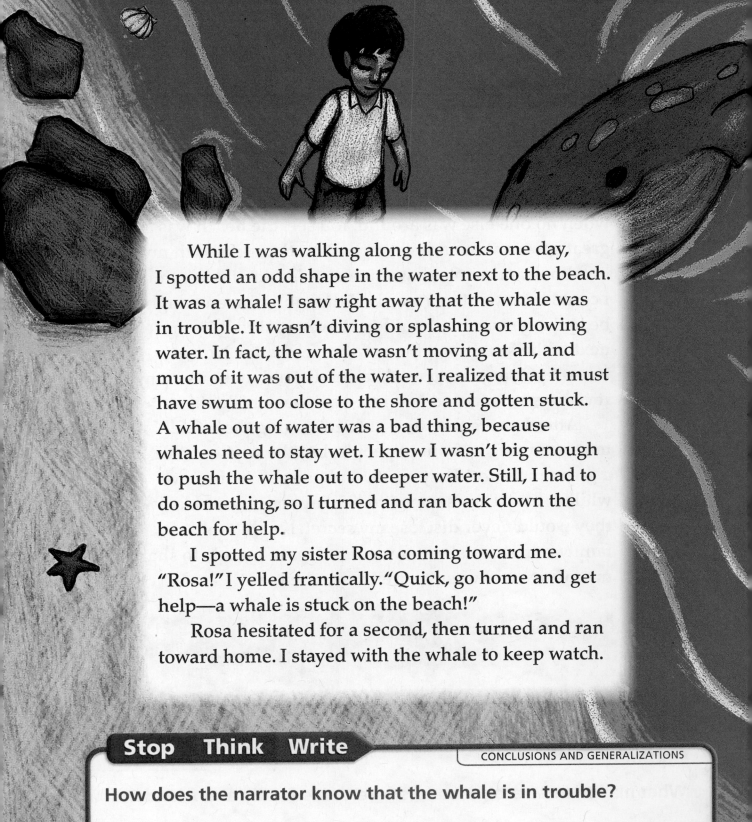

While I was walking along the rocks one day, I spotted an odd shape in the water next to the beach. It was a whale! I saw right away that the whale was in trouble. It wasn't diving or splashing or blowing water. In fact, the whale wasn't moving at all, and much of it was out of the water. I realized that it must have swum too close to the shore and gotten stuck. A whale out of water was a bad thing, because whales need to stay wet. I knew I wasn't big enough to push the whale out to deeper water. Still, I had to do something, so I turned and ran back down the beach for help.

I spotted my sister Rosa coming toward me. "Rosa!" I yelled frantically. "Quick, go home and get help—a whale is stuck on the beach!"

Rosa hesitated for a second, then turned and ran toward home. I stayed with the whale to keep watch.

Stop Think Write

CONCLUSIONS AND GENERALIZATIONS

How does the narrator know that the whale is in trouble?

_____

_____

_____

6

A few minutes later, my mom and dad came rushing toward me, with Rosa close on their heels. I showed them where the whale was, and we all walked toward it. Even though it was stuck, I could tell the whale was alive. It seemed to be watching us, and the air hole on top of its head moved as it breathed. Being so close to such a huge and powerful creature was scary, but also exciting. I hoped we could help it.

"We need to get this whale back in the sea!" Dad said. "Tomás, you and Rosa keep the whale wet while we run and get help."

Rosa and I waded into the water next to the whale and began to splash it.

"Oh, I wish the tide would hurry up and come in!" Rosa said.

I felt impatient, too, but I knew that the tide hurried for no one. "It won't be high tide for several hours," I told her. "We'll just have to wait."

Stop   Think   Write

UNDERSTANDING CHARACTERS

What do Tomás's and Rosa's actions tell you about them?

_____

_____

_____

The whale's look tormented me. Even though Rosa and I were keeping it wet, the whale was trembling with fear. I didn't see what else we could do to help it. Then I looked out at the other whales in the cove. They made me think of my songs and how much the whales seemed to like them. An idea took shape in my head.

"I'll sing to it!" I said to Rosa.

"You sing?" Rosa asked, shooting a puzzled glance at me.

At first I muted my voice and sang so quietly that I was making hardly any sound at all.

"Sing louder, Tomás. I think the whale is relaxing!" Rosa said.

So I sang louder. The whale *did* seem more relaxed. It wasn't trembling as much anymore, and a subtle twitch of its tail fin let me know that it was still alive. Rosa and I kept splashing the whale with water as I sang my songs.

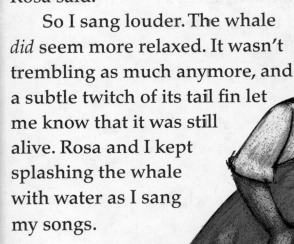

Stop   Think   Write

VOCABULARY

Why might Tomás have <u>muted</u> his voice to sing to the whale?

_____

_____

_____

8

A while later, we heard voices coming down the beach. My parents were back, and they were bringing help—lots of it, from what I could tell! It seemed as if the entire town had come to help save the whale.

I continued singing while everyone helped keep the whale wet. Whenever the whale started to shiver, I made my song softer to calm it down. I didn't think about the other people, or even look at them. I just thought about keeping the whale calm and alive until we could help it get to deeper water.

You know what? The more I sang, the calmer the whale seemed. The other whales in the cove seemed to be listening, too. They swam and splashed as they always did when I sang. I thought they might be watching and waiting for their friend to rejoin them.

Stop Think Write

UNDERSTANDING CHARACTERS

Why doesn't Tomás think about or look at the other people?

_____

_____

_____

At last the tide reached its highest point. The water lifted our whale from the sand, and it struggled out into the cove. I breathed a sigh of relief to see it swim off, safe and free.

As it joined the other whales, we all began to clap. It took me a moment to realize that the people around me didn't stop clapping when I did. With shock, I realized that they were now clapping for me!

"How on earth did you make up those amazing songs?" asked my mom.

When I described how I spent my time alone on the beach, my family was astonished.

"Keep writing your songs, Tomás," said my dad with pride. "Don't sing them just to save the whales," he added with a wry smile. "We'd like to hear them, too!"

I had thought it would be embarrassing to share my songs, but it made me feel good. In fact, it made me feel great!

"Okay," I agreed. "You've got a deal."

Stop Think Write

UNDERSTANDING CHARACTERS

Does Tomás's family like his songs? How can you tell?

_____

_____

_____

Look Back and Respond

1 How does Tomás feel about sharing his songs at the beginning of the story?

_____

_____

_____

Hint

For clues, look on pages 4 and 5.

2 How does Tomás change at the end of the story?

_____

_____

_____

Hint

For clues, look at pages 4, 5, 9, and 10.

3 Why does Tomás change his mind about singing his songs in front of other people?

_____

_____

_____

Hint

For clues, see page 10.

4 Why is Tomás shocked to realize that people are clapping for him?

_____

_____

_____

Hint

For clues, see pages 5 and 10.

Be a Reading Detective!

Return to

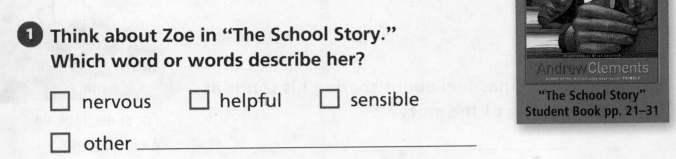

"The School Story"
Student Book pp. 21–31

1 Think about Zoe in "The School Story."
Which word or words describe her?

☐ nervous   ☐ helpful   ☐ sensible

☐ other _____

Prove It! What evidence in the story supports your answer?
Check the boxes. ☑ Make notes.

Evidence	Notes
☐ what Zoe says and does	
☐ what Natalie says and does	
☐ the illustrations	
☐	

Write About It!

UNDERSTANDING CHARACTERS

Answer question **1** using evidence from the text.

_____

_____

_____

_____

_____

_____

2 While she waits for her mom to read her book, Natalie starts to feel guilty. What causes her to feel this way?

☐ She knows her book is not good.

☐ She thinks of other writers whose books will never be read.

☐ She realizes her mother could get in trouble.

☐ other _____

Prove It! What evidence in the story supports your answer?
Check the boxes. ☑ Make notes.

Evidence	Notes
☐ all the envelopes in Ella's office	
☐ Natalie's thoughts and words	
☐ what Zoe says to Natalie	
☐	

Write About It!

CAUSE AND EFFECT

Answer question **2** using evidence from the text.

_____

_____

_____

_____

_____

_____

_____

✓ **TARGET VOCABULARY**

culprit
deprived
grimly
miraculous
pursuit

Turning Life Into Art

Some people write stories about their lives. Other people make movies or take photographs that document important personal events. People make sculptures and paintings about their experiences, too. Their lives become part of their

1 _____ of interesting and

beautiful art.

Even difficult situations can give you material for something creative. Let's say that your favorite pen disappears. You think someone might have taken it, and you search for the **2** _____. You may think **3** _____ of classmates who sit near your desk. It could turn out that you simply misplaced the pen, or that someone took it accidentally. Even so, you could write an intriguing mystery based on the experience, or make a painting about it.

People should not be **4** _____ of the opportunity to express themselves creatively. When you make a film or a series of photographs about something personal, the results can be amazing, or even **5** _____!

The Great Basketball Movie

by Richard Stull

"What are we going to do, Eddie?" asked Kenny.

Kenny and I were standing in the Middletown gym, watching our teammates practice basketball. Well, they were trying to practice. None of us really knew how to play basketball. In fact, none of us even liked basketball. However, for two days we had practiced, grimly determined to convince ourselves that we could play. How crazy could you get?

The madness started last week. That's when Middletown's inter-club games had been announced. The games were a school tradition that took place every year. Each after-school club was assigned to play some sort of sports game against another club. Usually, the game was no big deal. None of the clubs cared who won. We showed up for the game, had a little fun, and went home.

Stop Think Write

VOCABULARY

What does being <u>grimly</u> determined show about the team members?

_____

_____

_____

14

This year, though, things were different. The chosen sport was basketball. Our club, the Filmmaker's Club, was picked to play the Fantasy Sports Club. That's where the trouble began. We cared mostly about movies. We didn't think much about basketball. The kids in the Fantasy Sports Club were different. Even though they didn't all play basketball, they took sports seriously . . . very seriously.

The kids in Fantasy Sports knew a lot more about basketball than we ever would. A few of them were excellent players, too. They really wanted to win the game. Furthermore, they expected us to show up and play hard. They made it clear that they would consider anything less than a hard-fought game a form of treachery. They had no intention of being deprived of a meaningful victory.

Stop Think Write

MAIN IDEAS AND DETAILS

Do you think the game between the two clubs will be a close game? Give two details that support your thinking.

_____

_____

_____

15

I sighed. Kenny and I jogged out onto the gym floor to join the practice. Here we were, the five of us: Kenny, Ana, Jamal, Mai, and me, Eddie. I tossed the ball to Kenny. "Why don't you practice dribbling," I said.

Kenny started bouncing the ball across the floor. Mai covered her face with her hands. "No, Kenny," she shouted. "You have to use one hand to dribble, not two."

We were hopeless. There was no denying it. Nothing short of a miraculous game would save us. I decided that we needed a creative game plan—fast. I searched for some inspiration. I began to imagine the game as a scene in a movie I was directing. I wondered how I would approach the scene.

Stop   Think   Write

AUTHOR'S PURPOSE

Why do you think the author includes the scene of Kenny dribbling the basketball with two hands?

_____

_____

_____

Snap! In an instant I had an idea. We would turn our pathetic attempt to play a basketball game into a documentary film. I could see it in my mind. It would be the story of five ordinary kids sent cruelly to their doom on a basketball court. It would be a huge hit!

"Hey, everyone," I called out. "Come over for a huddle. I've got a great idea." My four teammates walked over. Mai pointed out that basketball players don't really huddle, but we did anyway.

"Okay," Kenny said. "What's your bright idea for making us a winning team?"

"Not a winning team," I said. "We're not even going to try to win. Instead, we're going to turn our loss into a documentary film about the losing team, us."

"A film about losers?" Jamal asked. "Hey, I kind of like the sound of that."

Stop   Think   Write

STORY STRUCTURE

What is Eddie's plan to help his team?

_____

_____

_____

17

"Won't the kids in Fantasy Sports get angry?" asked Mai. "If we don't even try, they're bound to blame us for robbing them of their moment of glory. I don't want them to see our team as the culprit."

"Maybe they won't be sore," I said. "After all, they'll be in the movie, too. At least this way, they'll get something exciting out of the game. Of course, I don't think we should tell them that we plan to lose."

"Yeah, let's not mention that point," Kenny agreed. "We'll just ask them if they want to be in the movie. They can accept or reject the idea."

Of course, the Fantasy members were delighted to be part of our movie. They imagined a thrilling saga of a hard-fought game between two evenly matched teams. In other words, they didn't know the truth.

Stop Think Write

CAUSE AND EFFECT

Why don't Eddie and his friends want to tell the members of Fantasy Sports that they plan to lose?

_____

_____

_____

18

I felt bad about what we were doing. I told myself that a little deception is often needed in pursuit of a good movie. Kenny loaded the camera, and we all got to work. We interviewed the kids in Fantasy Sports. They talked about how excited they were about the upcoming game. Then we interviewed each other. We talked about how important losing would be to each of us.

On the day of the game, Kenny's brother stood on the sidelines with the camera, filming the game. He got lots of great shots. He filmed Kenny putting up a one-handed shot into the wrong basket. He also shot Jamal grabbing the ball out of Ana's hands. I guess Jamal had forgotten that she was on our team.

Needless to say, the Fantasy Sports Club whipped us. The final score was 37–12. Afterward, I could tell that they were really angry. They felt we had embarrassed them by not taking the game seriously. It was hard to argue.

Stop   Think   Write

VOCABULARY

How do Eddie and his friends use deception in pursuit of a good movie?

_____

_____

_____

Later that week, we held a screening of our movie. Of course, we invited the kids in Fantasy.

Everyone sat silently while the film was screened. I must admit that I was impressed with our work. The movie was funny, with a lot of fake "serious" interviews with our teammates talking about how meaningful losing was to us. These were included with scenes from the game and scenes of the Fantasy Sports Club talking about winning.

With some great background music and funny titles, the film was a success. Even the members of Fantasy agreed. "I have to hand it to you," one of them said. "You may stink at basketball, but you sure make great movies."

The Fantasy Sports Club huddled together, and then they yelled out a cheer. "Let's hear it for the losers!" they shouted. It was music to my ears.

Stop Think Write

Why do you think the author ends the selection by having the Fantasy Sports Club cheer Eddie and his friends?

_____

_____

_____

Look Back and Respond

1 Why do you think the author wrote this story?

_____

_____

_____

Hint

What is the message of the story?

2 How would you describe Eddie?

_____

_____

_____

Hint

Clues appear on almost every page.

3 Why are the members of the Fantasy Sports Club angry after the basketball game?

_____

_____

_____

Hint

For clues, see pages 15, 18, and 19.

4 Do you think the author of "The Great Basketball Movie" approves of Eddie's plan? Explain.

_____

_____

_____

Hint

For clues, see pages 17 through 20.

21

Be a Reading Detective!

Return to

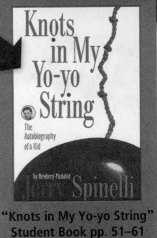

"Knots in My Yo-yo String"
Student Book pp. 51–61

1 **Jerry Spinelli writes that being a kid helped him as an author.** How does he explain this?

☐ He wrote his first novel when he was sixteen.

☐ Children are better writers than adults.

☐ He uses his childhood memories in his stories.

Prove It! What evidence in the selection supports your answer? Check the boxes. ☑ Make notes.

Evidence	Notes
☐ examples of Spinelli's work	
☐ Spinelli's childhood memories	
☐ details Spinelli gives about his life	
☐	

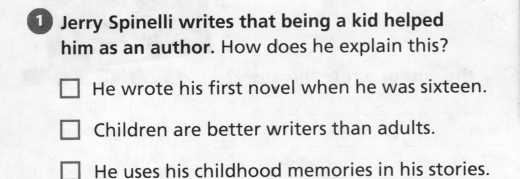

Write About It!

AUTHOR'S PURPOSE

Answer question **1** using evidence from the text.

_____

_____

_____

_____

_____

_____

_____

2 **What steps did Jerry Spinelli take in becoming a writer?** Write *1*, *2*, and *3* to show the order.

☐ He wrote *Space Station Seventh Grade,* a book about kids, and it was published.

☐ He took writing courses and became an editor.

☐ He wrote four novels that no one wanted to publish.

Prove It! What evidence in the selection supports your answer? Check the boxes. ☑ Make notes.

Evidence	Notes
☐ details about Spinelli's education and jobs	
☐ details Spinelli gives about his life	
☐ examples of Spinelli's work	

Write About It!

SEQUENCE OF EVENTS

Answer question 2 using evidence from the text.

_____

_____

_____

_____

_____

_____

_____

appealing
exploded
negotiations
painstaking
repetitive

Curl Up With a Good Book

Check the answer.

1 I have time to read this week. I am going to the library to choose a book that looks _____. I like a good fantasy with a hero quest.

☐ **pressuring** ☐ **wry** ☐ **appealing**

2 After finishing the _____ chores I must do every day, I have time to curl up by the fire with my new book. I am ready to be carried away to a world of wonder and daring.

☐ **deprived** ☐ **repetitive** ☐ **miraculous**

3 I love everything about reading a new book. I love the smell of the pages. I love the anticipation, wondering what will happen next. I even love the feeling of my muscles tensing as the main character makes a _____ decision that will have far-reaching consequences.

☐ **culprit** ☐ **disclose** ☐ **painstaking**

4 I can read for hours. Sometimes I think that even if something _____ right next to me, I would just keep on reading. Hours later, I would look up from the page to see a jumble of shattered glass and broken furniture all around me.

☐ **exploded** ☐ **appealing** ☐ **painstaking**

5 Tell about a time you were in <u>negotiations</u> with other members of your family to get something that mattered to you.

_____

_____

6 Tell about a time you had to make a <u>painstaking</u> decision.

_____

_____

7 Write an example of a <u>repetitive</u> activity.

_____

_____

All the Books in the World

by Jason Powe

How many books have you read? What if you had been born hundreds of years ago? Then you might have never even seen a book! Most people living then could not read. Few people owned even one book. Books were very hard to obtain. At that time, scribes had to copy every letter and every word by hand. ("Scribe" is an old word for someone who writes.) It took hundreds of hours to copy just one book.

Scribes often wrote on vellum, which came from animal skins. The results were **appealing**, beautiful, long-lasting books. Vellum was better than paper in some ways. It lasted longer than paper. That's a good thing! Old books written on vellum have taught us a lot about life long ago. So vellum helped preserve human history!

Stop Think Write

SUMMARIZE

How were books different hundreds of years ago?

_____

_____

_____

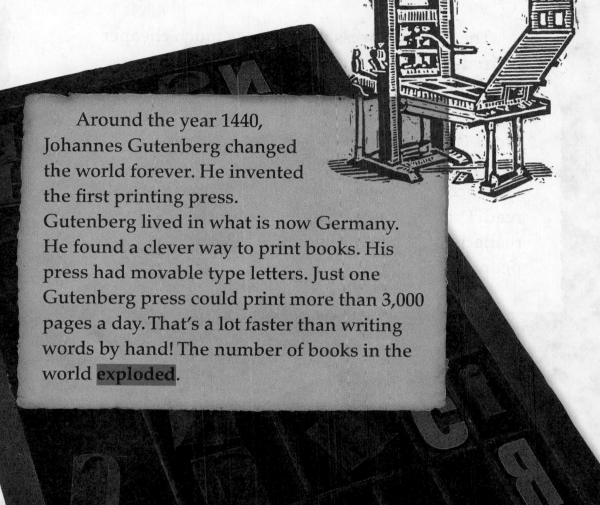

Around the year 1440, Johannes Gutenberg changed the world forever. He invented the first printing press. Gutenberg lived in what is now Germany. He found a clever way to print books. His press had movable type letters. Just one Gutenberg press could print more than 3,000 pages a day. That's a lot faster than writing words by hand! The number of books in the world exploded.

Stop   Think   Write

SEQUENCE OF EVENTS

What was the first big event that changed how books were made?

_____

_____

_____

The printing press made books much cheaper to produce. Printing became a **repetitive** process. One book could be produced over and over again mechanically. Because books were cheaper to make, they became cheaper to buy. Many people who had not previously had access to books could now own one. With access to books, many more people learned how to read. There was finally a good reason to become an avid reader! Publishers could afford to print books because people were buying them.

Stop Think Write

Why did the printing press make books cheaper to buy?

_____

_____

_____

Today, there are still many people in the world who don't have access to books. Some people have no books because they live in remote places. There are no stores that sell books in such areas. There may be no schools or libraries either. If you are looking for a special book, it can be hard to find. Very rare books can be found in just a few libraries on Earth. Getting hold of these books can be a **painstaking** process. There are many good reasons that people may not be able to obtain books that they want to read.

Stop Think Write

Why doesn't everyone in the world read books?

_____

_____

_____

In a short time, every person in the world may be able to find and read any book ever written. Imagine a remote village in Africa or Asia. That village may have no library buildings. It may have no bookstores. Now imagine that the village acquires a single computer—one with a virtual library.

For the cost of that one computer, every person in the village would have access to all the libraries in the world. A virtual library could have the same books as the largest libraries in major cities. The people in the village could read any books they wanted, without ever cracking a binding or turning a page!

Stop Think Write

How does the author want readers to feel about virtual libraries? How can you tell?

_____

_____

_____

The Internet is at the heart of this big idea. There are companies whose goal is to scan every book ever written into databases. Since 2004, over 15 million books have been scanned. Every day, thousands more books are made digital. The Internet makes books more widely available. It also helps to preserve the information in books.

In another ten years, it is possible that all of the world's 130 million books will be online. Millions of books can already be read online free of charge. To check them out, go online today!

Stop Think Write

CAUSE AND EFFECT

What is the second big event that has changed the way people read books?

_____

_____

_____

There is still one big problem to solve. It is based on a legal idea called "copyright." Look at the pages in the front of any book. You will see a copyright date and the publisher's name. Copyright laws protect the authors who write books and the publishers that print and sell books. A copyright gives publishers and writers a certain amount of time when no one can copy or sell their books without permission. Without copyrights, writers wouldn't be able to earn any money for their hard work.

Internet companies are in **negotiations** with authors, publishers, and the courts to find a fair way to pay for the books that are currently in print. In the future, people all over the world may be able to read almost every book ever written!

Stop   Think   Write

Why do copyright laws exist?

_____

_____

_____

Look Back and Respond

1 **Why were the first books expensive?**

_____

_____

_____

Hint

For clues, see page 24.

2 **List three facts from the selection about writing and reading.**

_____

_____

_____

Hint

Think about different ways books have been made and shared.

3 **Why are some books still hard to find?**

_____

_____

_____

Hint

For a clue, see page 27.

4 **How is the Internet changing the world of books?**

_____

_____

_____

Hint

For a clue, see page 29.

Be a Reading Detective!

Return to

The Making of a
BOOK
BY KAREN ROTHBART

"The Making of a Book"
Student Book pp. 79–89

1 In what order do these people work on a book?
Number them from *1* to *4*.

☐ agent

☐ author

☐ printer

☐ editor

Prove It! What evidence in the selection supports your answer?
Check the boxes. ☑   Make notes.

Evidence	Notes
☐ text about each person and what he or she does	
☐ the diagram on page 88	
☐ the subheads	

Write About It!

SEQUENCE OF EVENTS

Answer question **1** using evidence from the text.

_____

_____

_____

_____

_____

_____

_____

2 **In the late 1400s, the printing press was invented.** What conclusion can you draw about this invention?

☐ It made books too expensive for ordinary people.

☐ It made books affordable to the public.

☐ It slowed the process of publishing a book.

☐ other _____

Prove It! What evidence in the selection supports your answer? Check the boxes. ☑ Make notes.

Evidence	Notes
☐ details about printing	
☐ details about early books	
☐	

Write About It!

CONCLUSIONS AND GENERALIZATIONS

Answer question **2** using evidence from the text.

_____

_____

_____

_____

_____

_____

_____

_____

✓ **TARGET VOCABULARY**

accustomed
clustered
coaxed
urgent
void

Stories All Around

Check the answer.

1 Everyone has a story to tell, but we don't always take the time to listen. You might be _____ to saying hello to your neighbors, but have you taken the time to really get to know them?

☐ **clustered** ☐ **employed** ☐ **accustomed**

2 If you have a _____ in your day, you can fill the empty time by asking your neighbors about themselves.

☐ **void** ☐ **culprit** ☐ **coaxed**

3 People may be shy about sharing their stories at first. However, they may become more comfortable as you get to know them. Once people have been _____ into talking about themselves, they usually like it!

☐ **accustomed** ☐ **coaxed** ☐ **clustered**

4 Some people are bursting with stories that they just have to share! Someone might have an _____ need to talk about a particular experience or about a person who changed his or her life.

☐ **urgent** ☐ **revolting** ☐ **accustomed**

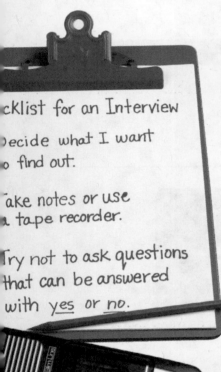

cklist for an Interview

Decide what I want
o find out.

ake notes or use
a tape recorder.

Try not to ask questions
that can be answered
with yes or no.

5 A good story always attracts a crowd. People might stand _____ around a storyteller, spellbound by the events the person describes.

☐ **employed** ☐ **accustomed** ☐ **clustered**

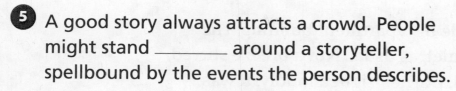

6 What are you <u>accustomed</u> to doing during your summer vacation?

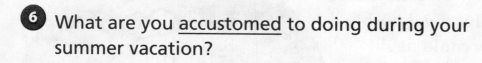
_____

_____

_____

7 What is an <u>urgent</u> request that someone might make?

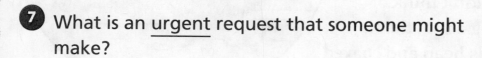
_____

_____

_____

8 Give an example of objects that might be <u>clustered</u> together.

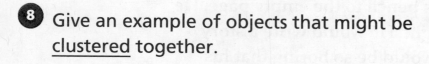
_____

_____

_____

On Duffield Street

by Claire Daniel

Darnell sat outside his apartment building. The neighborhood was quiet, as usual. Not a breeze stirred, and not a dog barked. Darnell sighed loudly. It was another boring day on Duffield Street.

To make matters worse, he had to write a story about his neighborhood for homework. How could he do that when nothing ever happened there? If there were kids around, Darnell might have more to write about, but all of his neighbors were adults. Darnell couldn't think of anything interesting about them.

He scratched his head and coaxed his brain to work, but no brilliant ideas came to him. He looked at his notebook page. It was whiter than white. He hadn't written a single word.

Darnell finally put his pencil to the empty page. He would write a story, all right. He would write a story about Duffield Street. It would be so boring that his teacher would fall asleep after reading the first page!

Stop Think Write

STORY STRUCTURE

What is Darnell's problem?

_____

_____

_____

Darnell saw his neighbor, Mr. Angelo, walking toward him. Every day, Mr. Angelo stopped on his way to his favorite café and tried to chat with Darnell. The old man always went on and on. Darnell usually said he had something urgent to do, because he didn't want to listen.

"Hi, Darnell," Mr. Angelo said. "What are you writing?"

"A story about the neighborhood," Darnell said. He hoped Mr. Angelo would keep walking, but he stopped.

"I have a million stories about this block!" Mr. Angelo said. "My favorite one is about my mother and father after they got married."

Darnell thought, "Here he goes again," but he didn't say the words out loud.

"My parents were born in Italy, but they met here in America," Mr. Angelo went on. "Then World War II started up, and Dad joined the army. My mom was all alone. It was lucky for her that she met Pauline."

Stop   Think   Write

VOCABULARY

Why does Darnell usually say he has something <u>urgent</u> to do when Mr. Angelo tries to talk to him?

_____

_____

_____

"Pauline? The lady who used to run the café?" Darnell asked. Pauline's had been on the block for as long as he could remember. The gray-haired lady who ran the place had retired just the year before. Now her son ran Pauline's.

Mr. Angelo nodded and said, "Yes, except Pauline's wasn't here when Mama and Papa came to this block. When Papa left, Mama was miserable. She felt a void in her life. She was accustomed to her large Italian family, and now she was alone with a little toddler to care for."

"You?" Darnell asked.

"Yes. Pauline saw how sad my mother was," Mr. Angelo went on. "The two became best friends. Then Pauline came up with a plan that changed their lives."

Stop   Think   Write

What was Mr. Angelo's mother's problem?

_____

_____

_____

"What was the plan?" Darnell asked. He leaned forward, listening closely. He could hardly believe it, but Angelo's story was actually interesting!

Mr. Angelo said, "Pauline came up with the idea of a restaurant. She was a very good cook, and so was my mother. They decided to start a business cooking large family meals for everyone in the neighborhood."

"Where was the restaurant?" Darnell asked.

"At first, they set up tables in Pauline's living room," said Mr. Angelo. "Then that got too crowded, so they decided to rent a space down at the end of the street. I think you know where that restaurant is!"

"The same place where Pauline's is now?" asked Darnell. "That's where you eat lunch every day, isn't it?"

"Right you are!" Mr. Angelo said, nodding. "On the very first day they opened, many people came to eat. The dining room was filled with diners! In short, Pauline's plan was a great success."

Stop Think Write

STORY STRUCTURE

How might Pauline's plan solve the problem that Mr. Angelo's mother had?

_____

_____

_____

"Then what happened?" Darnell asked.

"Well," said Mr. Angelo, "Mama always sang to herself while she worked. She had a lovely voice, and one day, Pauline asked her to sing for the customers. Mama picked out a few songs, and they hired a piano player. My mother became quite a hit. People started coming to the restaurant both to eat the good food and to hear my mother sing. Sometimes it was so crowded that people clustered in the doorway to hear Mama."

"Your mother must have been a very good singer," Darnell said.

"Oh, yes," Mr. Angelo said proudly.

"Your mother wasn't sad anymore about your dad being gone?" Darnell asked.

"She was a little sad," said Mr. Angelo. "I was very little, but I remember that she was busy all the time. She probably didn't have time to feel too alone."

Stop   Think   Write

Why were people <u>clustered</u> in the doorway of the restaurant?

_____

_____

_____

Mr. Angelo continued, "Mama loved singing, and she liked cooking the dinners because it was like cooking for her big family in Italy. The people in this neighborhood were like a new family to her. Then, when my father came home, my mother had a huge surprise. She had made a lot of money from the restaurant. She and Papa had enough to buy an apartment right on this block."

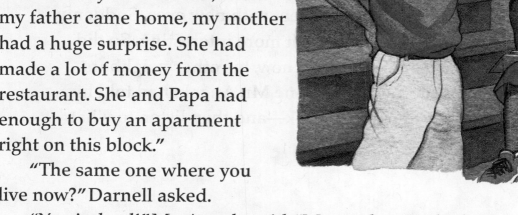

"The same one where you live now?" Darnell asked.

"Yes, indeed!" Mr. Angelo said. "My mother worked at Pauline's for many years. I like going there to eat because it's like eating Mama's home cooking."

"Mr. Angelo, that is a great story," Darnell said. "Why haven't you told it to me before?"

Darnell felt his face get hot. He knew the answer to his question. He had heard Mr. Angelo talk before, but he had never really listened to what he had to say.

Stop Think Write

INFER AND PREDICT

Why does Darnell's face feel hot?

_____

_____

_____

Mr. Angelo smiled at Darnell. "Any time you want a story," he said, "you know where to find one. I'll be glad to tell you anything you want to know."

Mr. Angelo continued walking toward Pauline's. After he left, Darnell sat down and began to write. His pencil moved quickly on the paper. When he was done, an idea came to him. Maybe he could talk to Pauline! She might have more to add to the story.

Darnell looked at his street with new eyes. Suddenly, Duffield Street seemed much more interesting. So did Mr. Angelo. For all Darnell knew, his other neighbors knew more stories like the one Mr. Angelo had told him. All Darnell had to do was ask—and then listen to what people told him.

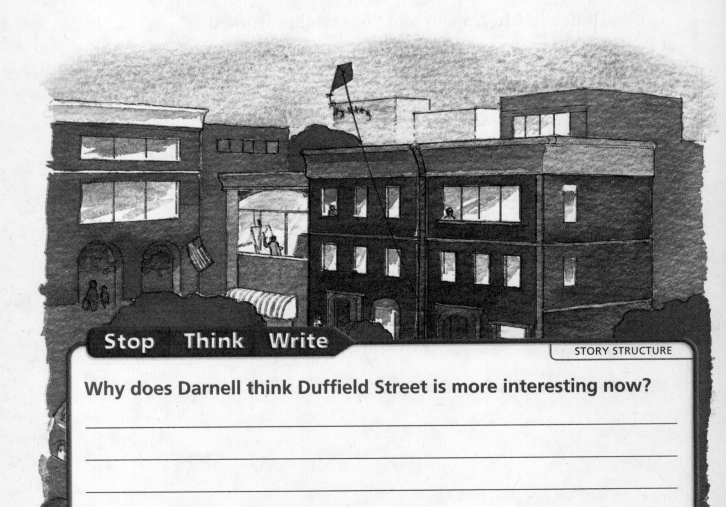

Stop   Think   Write

STORY STRUCTURE

Why does Darnell think Duffield Street is more interesting now?

_____

_____

_____

Look Back and Respond

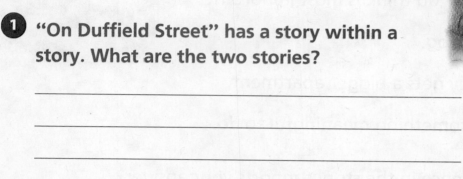

1 "On Duffield Street" has a story within a story. What are the two stories?

_____

_____

_____

Hint

Think about Darnell's situation. Think about what Mr. Angelo tells Darnell.

2 Who are the main characters in the story that Mr. Angelo tells Darnell?

_____

_____

_____

Hint

For clues, look on pages 36 and 37.

3 Why doesn't Darnell want to listen to Mr. Angelo in the beginning of the story?

_____

_____

_____

Hint

For clues, look on page 35.

4 How does Darnell change from the beginning of the story to the end?

_____

_____

_____

Hint

For clues, see pages 34 and 40.

Be a Reading Detective!

Return to

"The ACES Phone"
Student Book pp. 107–119

1 **Martin solves several problems in the story.**
Which solution do you think is most important?

☐ Martin gets a dog.

☐ Martin's family gets a bigger apartment.

☐ Martin finds something meaningful to do.

Prove It! What evidence in the story supports your answer?
Check the boxes. ☑ Make notes.

Evidence	Notes
☐ Martin's feelings at the beginning	
☐ Martin's feelings at the end	
☐	

Write About It!

STORY STRUCTURE

Answer question **1** **using evidence from the text.**

_____

_____

_____

_____

_____

_____

_____

2 **The author's main purpose in "The ACES Phone" is to entertain. What is another of the author's reasons for writing this story?**

☐ to encourage people to treat pets well

☐ to show that things get worse before they get better

☐ to suggest that young and old can never get along

Prove It! What evidence in the story supports your answer? Check the boxes. ☑ Make notes.

Evidence	Notes
☐ what Mrs. D says	
☐ what the landlord says	
☐ Martin's feelings listening to the phone	
☐ the illustrations	

Write About It!

AUTHOR'S PURPOSE

Answer question 2 using evidence from the text.

_____

_____

_____

_____

_____

_____

41B

Becoming a Comedian

TARGET VOCABULARY

aspect
credit
genuinely
tendency
tension

If you're thinking of becoming a comedian, there's a lot to consider. Telling funny jokes is only one ❶ _____ of the job. Presenting your material well is also important. So is finding an audience!

Being ❷ _____ funny is a gift. It isn't easy to be a comedian if being funny doesn't come to you naturally. Humor isn't really something you can learn, like spelling.

Many comedians borrow or adapt ideas from past comedians. There's nothing wrong with this. Comedians usually give

3 _____ to people whose work has influenced them.

When a joke falls flat, a quick recovery is important. Even if the comedian feels a lot of

4 _____, it shouldn't show. Sometimes it's easiest to simply say something like, "Wow, I can't believe I tried to get away with that rubbish!"

Remember this. People in the audience have a

5 _____ to laugh when they listen to a comedian. They want to have fun. The audience isn't your enemy!

The Comedian

by D. J. Ortiz

"Do you know what the dinosaur said to the chicken?" Emilio asked.

The young children who were gathered around him looked shy. They also looked embarrassed. They were silent as stones. I felt some tension in the air. I'm Emilio's sister, and I know he wants to be a comedian.

"Oh, come on, take a guess!" he pleaded.

"What did the dinosaur say?" one little girl said.

"You look like dinner to me!" Emilio said. He laughed.

The three children simply stared at him. They began drifting away, heading for other parts of the playground.

"Did I say something wrong?" Emilio asked me.

I stared at his costume. His hair was covered with a black wig, and he wore a mustache, a big suit, and a tie. "I think I can answer your question," I told him.

Stop   Think   Write

SUMMARIZE

What is Emilio's problem?

_____

_____

_____

"Well?" Emilio said.

"Do you really want to become a comedian?"

"You know that I do. Too bad I can't even make a group of second graders laugh. I stink worse than a skunk convention," Emilio said.

"You're not that bad," I said. "I could give you some pointers—that is, if you'll listen to me."

"I'm listening, with all twelve ears."

"You don't have twelve ears," I said.

"Ha, ha, ha!" Emilio laughed. "I meant twelve years!"

"Stop right there," I said. "You have a tendency to laugh at your own jokes. Rule number one is no laughing at your own jokes."

"Why not?" asked Emilio, clearly puzzled.

I sighed and shook my head. "If the joke is funny, other people will laugh. No one will laugh just because you do."

Stop Think Write

VOCABULARY

What is Emilio's _tendency_ after he tells a joke?

_____

_____

_____

45

"All right," Emilio said, "that's rule number one. What's rule number two?"

As patiently as possible, I said, "You have to start with the basics. You need to get your own material. Think of a theme or a story, and then use it to tell several jokes."

"What kind of theme do you mean?" he asked.

"Use your imagination," I replied. I suggested that he choose something ordinary, like dogs or baseball. I also said he could write about something as common as a watch or time. "The important thing," I said, "is to think up something that anyone can relate to."

Emilio seemed to be listening to me, and he went right to work. The next day he was ready with his new material. He said, "This new routine is going to make you laugh hysterically."

Stop Think Write

CAUSE AND EFFECT

Why is it important for a comedian to think of things that people can relate to?

_____

_____

_____

I waited patiently. I was ready to give him **credit** for his new material.

Emilio said, "Do you know the difference between a ship captain and a jeweler? The ship captain watches the sea, and the jeweler sees the watch. Do you know why the guy got rid of his watchdog? Because the dog couldn't tell time. The same guy threw his alarm clock out the window just to see time fly."

I just sat there without a trace of a smile on my face. I couldn't pretend his jokes were funny. If anything, I felt a bit annoyed. "I think those are the worst jokes I've ever heard," I said. "Did you really make those up?"

Emilio said, "I did what you said. I looked on the Internet. I found these jokes about a watch and a dog and telling time. You said I should do a theme."

"The best comedians don't use other people's jokes," I said. "They make them up!"

Stop Think Write

FACT AND OPINION

Emilio's sister says, "The best comedians don't use other people's jokes." Is this a fact or an opinion? Explain.

_____

_____

_____

"Oh, never mind," Emilio said. "I'm never going to be a comedian. I was no good at soccer. I can't spell very well. Let's face it, I'm the worst card in the pack."

I gave him a pat on the back. "No, you're not. I'm sure you will be successful. By the time I get through with you, you'll be the joker. You'll have people in stitches."

Emilio groaned, and I added, "What you need to do is make jokes about some aspect of your own life. You could tell about going to school or taking a family vacation. Or you could tell about the people you know. Think of your favorite comedians. They all make jokes about people they know."

"Okay, okay," Emilio said with more enthusiasm. "There's no lack of material in my life. I've got more material than a dress factory!"

"You're funnier when you don't try so hard," I said. "Get at it and write, big brother." To my surprise, he did.

Stop Think Write

VOCABULARY

What is an aspect of Emilio's life that he could write about?

_____

_____

_____

A few days later, Emilio had a routine ready. He tried out his new jokes on me. Maybe I didn't laugh, but I did smile. "Not bad," I said. "You have a few days to practice before my birthday party on Sunday."

"You think I'm ready for that?" he asked.

"The real question is, are we ready for you?" I said.

Everybody came on Sunday—aunts, uncles, grandparents, cousins. After dinner, I said, "I'd like to present Emilio, the Joker!" The family clapped politely.

Emilio cleared his throat. "I decided to become a comedian," he said, "because I'm not good at much else. I'm terrible at school. I was really happy that my last report card was terrible."

"Why were you happy?" I called out.

"Because at least Mom and Dad knew it was mine," Emilio said. Dad let out a guffaw, and I heard some laughter.

Stop   Think   Write

INFER AND PREDICT

Why does the family clap politely when Emilio's sister introduces him?

_____

_____

_____

Emilio said, "My parents think I should be like my relatives, but I'm not so sure. Take Uncle Luis. He makes those great pickles. Everyone loves them. So what? Why is a pickle such a big dill?" Uncle Luis let out a hoot.

Everyone laughed. "Good one," said Mom.

"I really wanted to be a good speller," Emilio said. "I tried everything. I wrote my spelling words over and over. I sang them in the shower. Finally, I swallowed a dictionary."

"How did it taste?" Uncle Luis asked.

"Educational," Emilio said. "My sister kept asking me if it helped, but I didn't say a thing. She wasn't getting a word out of me."

The family was **genuinely** impressed. Everyone clapped and laughed. Maybe there was hope for my brother after all.

Stop Think Write

STORY STRUCTURE

Why is the family surprised by Emilio's act?

_____

_____

_____

Look Back and Respond

1 Who is Emilio's first audience in the story?

_____

_____

_____

Hint

For a clue, see page 44.

2 When Emilio's sister says, "You're funnier when you don't try so hard," is she stating a fact or an opinion? How can you tell?

_____

_____

_____

Hint

Remember, an opinion is what someone thinks or believes.

3 How has Emilio changed during the story?

_____

_____

_____

Hint

Clues can be found on all pages.

4 How do people react to Emilio's jokes at the beginning of the story? How do they react to his jokes at the end of the story?

_____

_____

_____

Hint

For clues, see pages 44 and 50.

Be a Reading Detective!

"The Myers Family"
Student Book pp. 137–145

1 **Is the following statement a fact or an opinion?**
The work that Walter and Christopher Myers do
is easier for them because they are related.

☐ It is a fact.

☐ It is an opinion.

Prove It! What evidence in the selection supports your answer?
Check the boxes. ☑ Make notes.

Evidence	Notes
☐ Walter's words and actions	
☐ Christopher's words and actions	
☐ how publishers feel and act	

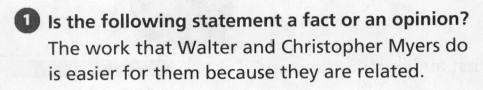

Write About It!

FACT AND OPINION

Answer question **1** using evidence from the text.

_____

_____

_____

_____

_____

_____

2 As a child, did Christopher Myers get much encouragement for his art?

☐ No, his father didn't notice Christopher's ability.

☐ Yes, his family encouraged him.

☐ other _____

Prove It! What evidence in the selection supports your answer? Check the boxes. ☑ Make notes.

Evidence	Notes
☐ what his mother did with his drawings	
☐ what his father said about his first published drawing	
☐ art contests he won as a child	
☐	

Write About It!

MAIN IDEA AND DETAILS

Answer question **2** using evidence from the text.

_____

_____

_____

_____

_____

_____

_____

**flair
fundamental
lingered
phenomenal
showdown**

Early Radio Shows

Radio was a **①** _____ invention that captured people's imaginations. Thousands of people wanted to experiment with this amazing new technology.

Until late 1912, there were no laws regulating radio transmitters in the United States. People with a **②** _____ for mechanical things could set up stations wherever they wished. These amateurs, known as "hams," were free to broadcast anything they wished, from wherever they happened to be.

In 1912, there was a 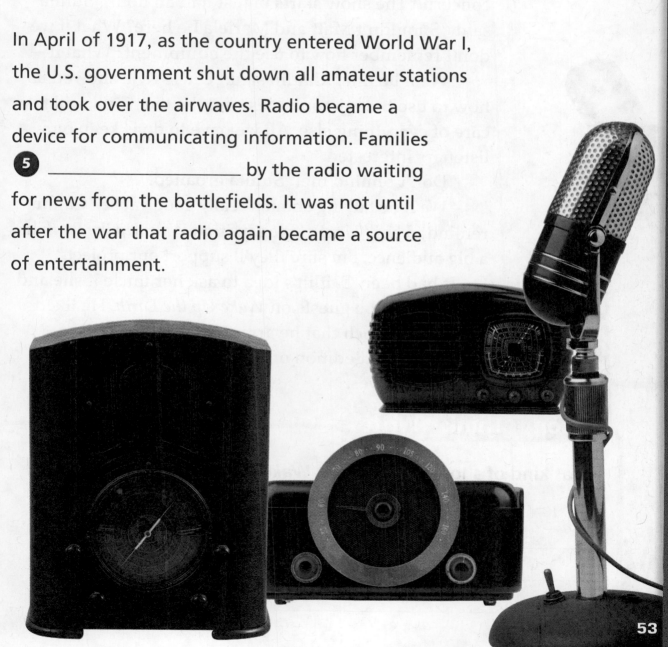 **3** _____ between the radio operators and the government. The government passed new rules setting limits on who could send radio signals. This led to a basic, or **4** _____, change in the way radio shows were made.

In April of 1917, as the country entered World War I, the U.S. government shut down all amateur stations and took over the airwaves. Radio became a device for communicating information. Families **5** _____ by the radio waiting for news from the battlefields. It was not until after the war that radio again became a source of entertainment.

The Green Machine

by Dina McClellan

When Caitlin got to the WUHA radio station, Sunita was already there. She jumped up, her face filled with concern. "The show starts in just half an hour," Sunita said. "Shouldn't Matt and Mariela be here? What if we don't remember how to use the equipment? What if—"

"We'll be fine," Caitlin said. "Uncle Kyle showed us how to use the microphones, and the tech crew will take care of everything else. All we have to do is keep our listeners interested."

"Don't remind me!" Sunita groaned.

"We'll be talking about a really good cause," Caitlin reminded her. "Uncle Kyle says that *Wake Up the Earth* has a big audience. I'm sure they'll support our project."

It had been Caitlin's idea to ask her uncle if she and Sunita could be guests on *Wake Up the Earth*. He liked the idea so much that he arranged for them to do a special student edition of the show that they would host themselves.

Stop   Think   Write

INFER/PREDICT

What kind of show do you think *Wake Up the Earth* is?

_____

_____

_____

The girls didn't have any more time to worry. Mariela and Matt arrived, and before they knew it, the four of them were in the studio. Caitlin's uncle signaled to them from the booth. Then the ON AIR sign flashed red, and they were on.

"Good afternoon!" Sunita chirped nervously into the microphone. "I'm Sunita Tejani."

"And I'm Caitlin Ratliffe. We're here to host a special student edition of *Wake Up the Earth*."

"We have an awesome show for you today," Sunita said. "Our guests are Matt Reid and Mariela Guzman. They've formed a new group at our school, and they're planning amazing work."

Sunita was already sounding a little calmer. Caitlin smiled at her, and then said to Mariela and Matt, "Why don't you tell our listeners about what you're up to?"

Stop   Think   Write

UNDERSTANDING CHARACTERS

Why do you think Sunita is nervous?

_____

_____

_____

"Matt and I started the Green Machine because we saw a fundamental problem at Greenwood Middle School and we wanted to do something about it," Mariela began.

"The school's appearance is pretty bad," Matt added. "The field is like a dust pit—there's almost no grass. There are holes in the fence, and the bushes in front of the school are dead because of some plant disease."

Sunita leaned forward and said into the microphone, "Why didn't the school do something about these problems?"

"Well, our teachers and principal are great," said Matt. "However, with recent cuts in the school budget, there's not a lot of money for extras like landscaping."

Mariela had a photograph of the school with her. She put it on the table and said, "The school grounds have gotten so bad that some kids started leaving trash around."

Stop Think Write

What **fundamental** problem do Matt and Mariela want to solve at their school?

_____

_____

_____

"What can the Green Machine do to make things better?" Caitlin asked.

"For starters, we'd like to fix the fence, plant new grass, and get some new bushes to replace the dead ones," Matt explained. "Then maybe kids will stop littering."

Caitlin took a deep breath. Matt had just given her the cue to make her pitch for help. "I'm sure there must be people in our audience who can support the Green Machine," she said. "Listeners, if you have some extra grass seed, the Green Machine could use it!"

Sunita chimed in with requests for donations to mend the school's fence and plant new bushes. Then, after thanking their guests, Sunita and Caitlin ended the show.

"You two really have a flair for radio!" Matt said.

Sunita and Caitlin grinned at each other. "Now comes the hard part," said Caitlin. "Waiting to see what kind of response we get!"

Stop Think Write

THEME

How are Sunita and Caitlin trying to help the Green Machine?

_____

_____

_____

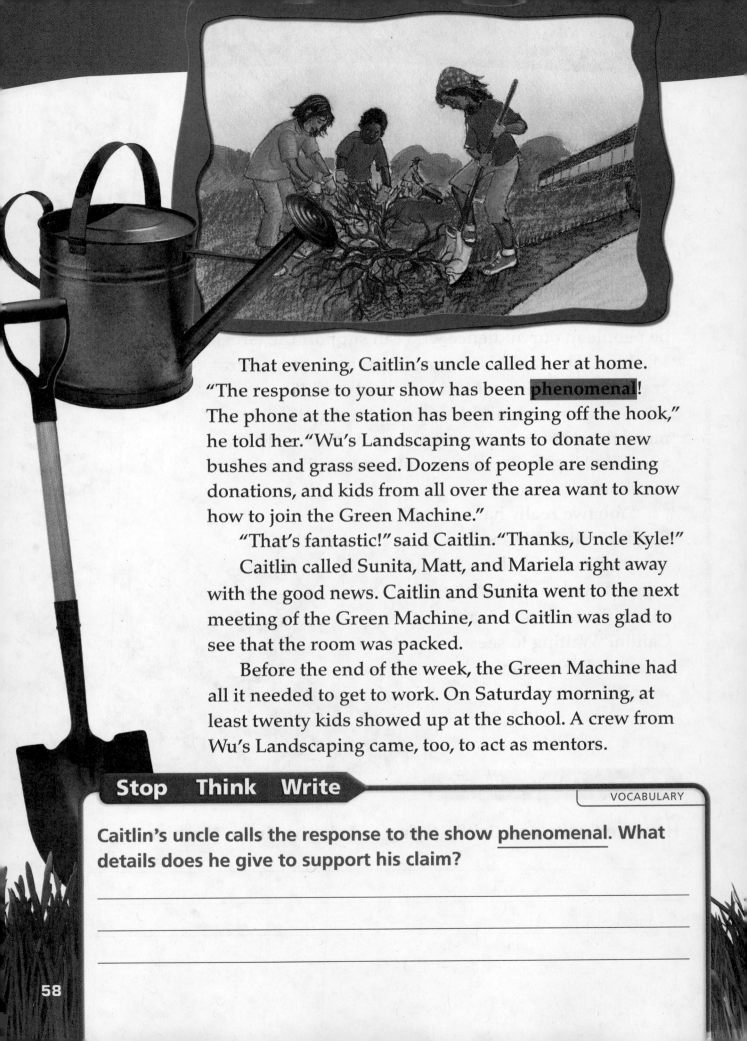

That evening, Caitlin's uncle called her at home. "The response to your show has been **phenomenal**! The phone at the station has been ringing off the hook," he told her. "Wu's Landscaping wants to donate new bushes and grass seed. Dozens of people are sending donations, and kids from all over the area want to know how to join the Green Machine."

"That's fantastic!" said Caitlin. "Thanks, Uncle Kyle!"

Caitlin called Sunita, Matt, and Mariela right away with the good news. Caitlin and Sunita went to the next meeting of the Green Machine, and Caitlin was glad to see that the room was packed.

Before the end of the week, the Green Machine had all it needed to get to work. On Saturday morning, at least twenty kids showed up at the school. A crew from Wu's Landscaping came, too, to act as mentors.

Stop Think Write

Caitlin's uncle calls the response to the show phenomenal. What details does he give to support his claim?

_____

_____

_____

Caitlin could hardly believe how much they accomplished in a single day. One crew went around with garbage bags and cleaned up trash. Mr. Wu directed a second group as they dug up dead bushes and planted new ones. His son showed a third group of students how to sprinkle grass seeds.

"This field will be covered with lush, green grass before you know it," said Mr. Wu.

Caitlin felt proud when the principal came by to thank them for all their hard work. Everyone clapped when he put up a sign that read, "This project completed by THE GREEN MACHINE." Caitlin, Sunita, Mariela, and Matt lingered at the school after the others left. They were amazed by how different—and how much nicer—their school looked now.

Stop Think Write

THEME

Tell how the Green Machine crews are able to complete the project in one day.

_____

_____

_____

59

A week later, Caitlin, Sunita, Matt, and Mariela were back on the air at WUHA.

"Before we begin this week's episode of *Wake Up the Earth*, we want to thank our listeners for their response to last week's show," Sunita said into the microphone.

The four students briefly talked about the donations they had received and the work the Green Machine had done at the school. Then Caitlin asked, "What's next for the Green Machine?"

"We're getting ready for a showdown with town officials," Matt said. "The town closed a local playground, but we think it should be fixed up and reopened. Kids in the neighborhood need a place to play."

Sunita looked at the photograph that Mariela held up. "You've got your work cut out for you," Sunita said. "However, if anyone can do it, the Green Machine can."

Stop   Think   Write

THEME

Why do you think the four students talk about the Green Machine's new project on the next radio show?

_____

_____

_____

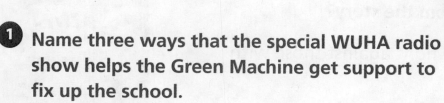

Look Back and Respond

1 Name three ways that the special WUHA radio show helps the Green Machine get support to fix up the school.

_____

_____

_____

Hint

For clues, see page 58.

2 Tell how the kids and Wu's landscaping crew help one another get the job done in one day.

_____

_____

_____

Hint

For clues, see page 59.

3 What is the theme, or main lesson, that the author wants readers to understand? Explain.

_____

_____

_____

Hint

Think about what the four students learn.

4 What do you think will be the result of the showdown between the Green Machine and town officials? Explain.

_____

_____

_____

Hint

Think about how well the Green Machine's plan to fix up the school worked.

Be a Reading Detective!

Return to

The Boy Who Saved Baseball

JOHN H. RITTER

"The Boy Who Saved Baseball"
Student Book pp. 167–179

1 **What message about life does the author want readers to learn from the story?**

☐ It's pointless to fight against those with more power.

☐ Always act out of good intentions rather than fear.

☐ Computer games are a good way to learn baseball.

Prove It! What evidence in the story supports your answer? Check the boxes. ☑ Make notes.

Evidence	Notes
☐ what Tom's friends say	
☐ what adults in the story say	
☐ Tom's thoughts at the end of the story	

Write About It!

THEME

Answer question **1** **using evidence from the text.**

_____

_____

_____

_____

_____

_____

_____

2 **Why does Tom consider not playing his best in the big game?**

☐ He doesn't think the Wildcats have a chance of winning.

☐ He thinks the people of the town will suffer if the Wildcats win.

☐ He thinks Alabaster Jones's plans will improve the town.

☐ other _____

Prove It! What evidence in the story supports your answer?
Check the boxes. ☑ Make notes.

Evidence	Notes
☐ what Jones says	
☐ how Tom feels as Jones speaks	
☐ Tom's thoughts after the conversation	
☐	

Write About It!

CAUSE AND EFFECT

Answer question 2 using evidence from the text.

_____

_____

_____

_____

_____

_____

_____

✔ TARGET VOCABULARY

correspond
distinguish
impressive
intriguing
observe

KNOTS

Knots have been in use for thousands of years. They are used for recording information, for decoration, and for tying things together. When a knot is used for holding things together, the type of knot must **correspond** to the type of thing being tied. For example, some knots are used to tie a rope to an object. Others are used to tie different objects together.

Many knots look very similar, so it is important to carefully **observe** how the knot is tied. You must **distinguish** between two knots that look similar. Often, a knot that is not tied correctly will fail under pressure.

Knots are also used for their appearance and decorative value. A single knot can be used to braid portions of a string into a long and **impressive**-looking friendship bracelet. Bracelets can also be made by repeating one kind of knot over and over.

When a cord is entangled, there may be knots in the cord. It is also possible that there is no knot at all! Magicians sometimes use this fact in a trick. The idea that a knot that looks firm can be "magically" untied is **intriguing** to an audience.

1 A knot tied in a heavy rope would

_____ well to a need to tie a

ship to a dock. By contrast, a decorative knot tied

with shiny ribbon is a good match with a need to

make a gift look festive.

2 If you wanted to learn how to tie a knot, it would

be more useful to _____ the

hands than the feet of the person tying the knot.

3 Do you find the topic of knots intriguing? Why or
why not?

_____

_____

4 Describe something you find impressive.

_____

_____

5 Name a time when it is important to carefully
distinguish between two things that are very
similar.

_____

_____

All Tied Up

By Jack Beers

Have you ever pulled your MP3 player out of a bag or pocket and found the wires hopelessly tangled? Sometimes ropes and wires find a way to get knotted and entangled, even when they are left alone. Knots develop in the strands of many different materials. They even occur within our own bodies.

Knots can be beneficial to humans, or they can be harmful. There are thousands of different ways for people to tie things with knots. Scientists and mathematicians have also studied knots in the natural world. In the process, they have discovered that knots can cause problems for living things. But living things also have ways to untie knots that occur naturally within their bodies.

Stop Think Write

CITE TEXT EVIDENCE

Do knots occur solely as a result of humans tying them? Explain.

_____

_____

_____

Knots Tied by Humans

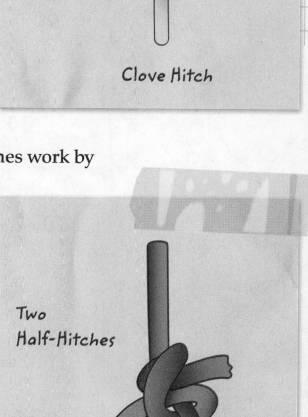

Clove Hitch

Two Half-Hitches

Although there are thousands of different knots used by humans, they can be categorized by the purpose for which they are used. A *hitch* is a knot that is used to tie a rope to an object. Some hitches work by tying the rope around the object. Some work by tying the rope around itself. A Clove Hitch, for example, uses two loops called half-hitches to attach the rope to a bar. The Two Half-Hitches knot also uses two half-hitches, but they are wrapped around the rope. Look at the drawings of the two knots. How can you **distinguish** one knot from the other?

Some hitches are meant to allow the rope to be tightened after the knot is tied. The Tautline Hitch can be tightened by pulling the finished knot away from the bar to which it is attached.

Stop   Think   Write

TEXT AND GRAPHIC FEATURES

How is the Clove Hitch different from the Two Half-Hitches? Use the pictures to answer the question.

_____

_____

_____

Bowline
(loose)

Single-loop knots are knots that produce a loop in the rope. The loop will not close after the knot is tightened. The most popular and well known of these knots is the Bowline, which is known as the "King of Knots." Having a loop that will not close is useful for mountain climbing. It also allows a rope to be attached to an object or another rope in many different ways.

After they **observe** how a knot is tied, knot lovers often use a familiar saying to remember how to tie the knot. For the Bowline, there is a way that knot tiers remember what to do after making the initial loop. They "send the rabbit (the end of the rope) out of its hole, around the tree, and back into the hole."

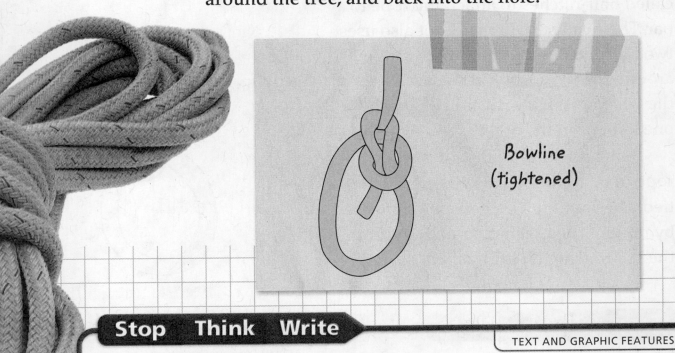

Bowline
(tightened)

Stop Think Write

What does it mean to "send the rabbit out of its hole, around the tree, and back into the hole"?

_____

_____

_____

Sometimes two lengths of rope need to be tied together to make a longer rope. That is when a *bend* comes in handy. One of the simplest bends to tie is the Alpine Butterfly Bend. This knot is tied by looping each rope around the other rope and bringing the two ends through the center of the knot. Notice in the drawing that each rope is tied as a mirror-image of the way in which the other rope is tied.

Alpine Butterfly Bend

A knot like the Alpine Butterfly Bend is easy to remember because it doesn't matter whether the ends of the rope are curved upward or downward. It only matters that the knot is tied in the same manner. If the ropes are different thicknesses, other types of bends work better. But usually when a simple knot like this one holds well, it is a good choice.

Stop Think Write

TEXT AND GRAPHIC FEATURES

How does the picture help you understand how to tie an Alpine Butterfly Bend?

_____

_____

_____

Knots are also used in craft projects. In making crafts, a single pattern can be used over and over to create a whole. Turk's Head knots use a repeated knot pattern called an Overhand Knot to create an **impressive** design that can be worn as a bracelet. The simple Reef Knot, often known as a Square Knot, can be used repeatedly to tie a Dragonfly. A repeated braid between the end of a rope and a loop of the rope will make a Braid Knot that can be long or short. The repeating patterns in knots can be interesting and even beautiful.

Turk's Head

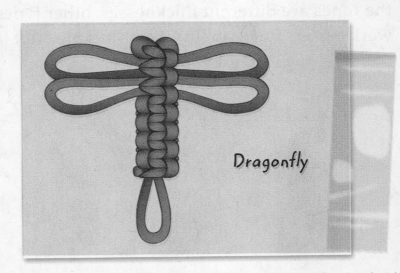

Dragonfly

Stop   Think   Write

MAIN IDEA AND DETAILS

Why are knots used for crafts?

_____

_____

_____

Knots Inside Humans

Molecules that are long and slender tend to get twisted and form knots. Probably the most important of these are strands of DNA. These are the molecules that contain the genetic information that tells living things how to function.

DNA is acted on by enzymes that copy its information. The problem is that DNA is tightly packed into cells. This is called supercoiling. The enzymes that act on DNA to copy it first have to straighten it out somewhat. They do this by snipping parts of the DNA where they cross. The ends of each cut strand are rejoined to the ends that **correspond** to them. The result is a strand that is less coiled. Also, when strands of DNA get knotted, the enzymes are able to untangle the DNA at its crossings. It is **intriguing** to think that our bodies, unlike our MP3 players, have built-in methods of untying knots that occur.

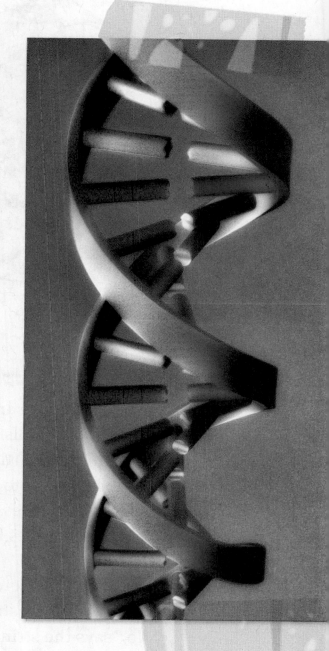

Stop Think Write

VOCABULARY

Name something that you find _intriguing_ about DNA.

_____

_____

_____

Knots and Wordplay

Finally, knots are an endless source of jokes and wordplay in the English language. It would simply knot be right to end this article without one knotty joke.

A string walks into a diner and orders a burger. "I'm sorry," says the waitress, "but we don't serve strings here." The string goes home, messes up its hair, and ties itself in a knot.

Then the string returns to the diner. The waitress says, "Aren't you the string that was here an hour ago?"

"No," says the string. "I'm a frayed knot."

Stop Think Write

CONCLUSIONS AND GENERALIZATIONS

Are knots more beneficial or more harmful to humans? Why do you think so?

_____

_____

_____

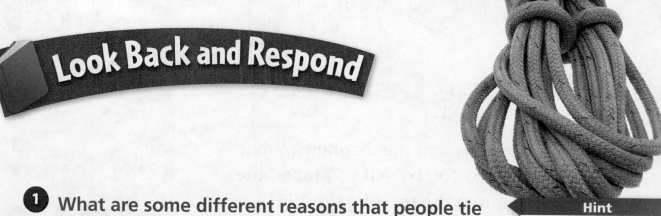

Look Back and Respond

1 What are some different reasons that people tie knots in ropes?

_____
_____
_____

Hint

For clues, see pages 65, 66, and 67.

2 What are some ways that knots are used in crafts?

_____
_____
_____

Hint

For a clue, see page 68.

3 Why are there different knots designed for the same purpose?

_____
_____
_____

Hint

For clues, see pages 65 and 67.

4 In nature, how can one particular kind of knot be "untied"?

_____
_____
_____

Hint

For a clue, see page 69.

Be a Reading Detective!

Return to

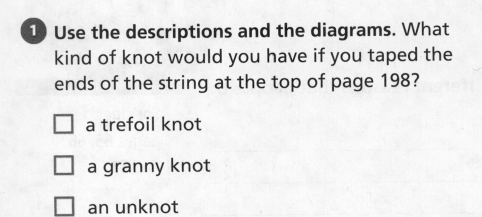

"Do Knot Enter"
Student Book pp. 197–205

1 **Use the descriptions and the diagrams.** What kind of knot would you have if you taped the ends of the string at the top of page 198?

☐ a trefoil knot

☐ a granny knot

☐ an unknot

☐ other _____

Prove It! What evidence in the selection supports your answer? Check the boxes. ☑ Make notes.

Evidence	Notes
☐ knots on pages 199 and 201	
☐ text on pages 200 and 201	
☐	

Write About It!

TEXT AND GRAPHIC FEATURES

Answer question ❶ using evidence from the text.

_____

_____

_____

_____

_____

_____

_____

2 **What is the author's purpose on page 205?**

☐ to describe how DNA works

☐ to explain how knot theory applies to the human body

☐ to show the difference between biology and math

☐ other _____

Prove It! What evidence in the selection supports your answer?
Check the boxes. ☑ Make notes.

Evidence	Notes
☐ the heading	
☐ details about how DNA can form knots	
☐ what biologists and mathematicians hope to do	

Write About It!

AUTHOR'S PURPOSE

Answer question 2 using evidence from the text.

_____

_____

_____

_____

_____

_____

TARGET VOCABULARY

complex
elegant
principle
reluctant
specimens

School Science Fairs

Check the answer.

1 A display in a science fair might demonstrate a scientific _____.

☐ **mentor**   ☐ **principle**   ☐ **elegant**

2 Sometimes a simple display may beat a more _____ display.

☐ **reluctant**   ☐ **literary**   ☐ **complex**

3 Display all the _____ that you have gathered for your display.

☐ **transmissions**   ☐ **specimens**   ☐ **principle**

4 Try to find an _____ way to explain a complicated idea.

☐ **elegant**   ☐ **aspect**   ☐ **reluctant**

5 Don't be _____ to try something new!

☐ **brainwashed**   ☐ **elegant**   ☐ **reluctant**

6 What is the most <u>complex</u> task that you do every day? Explain.

_____

_____

_____

7 What chores are you <u>reluctant</u> to do? Explain.

_____

_____

_____

8 Name a <u>principle</u> that you think a politician should follow.

_____

_____

_____

A Prize to DYE For!

by Shirley Granahan

Hi, I'm Josie, and I love being a winner. Lucky for me, I'm the fastest runner on my block. I know that to be the best, you have to train and keep in shape. So I practice every day. I definitely don't like to lose!

Not to brag or anything, but I'm also the best speller in school. I won the spelling bee last year. I'm the best at math and science, too. It takes hard work to be the best, so I spend a lot of time alone, studying.

Once a year, however, I'm pretty popular. Our school has a science fair. All the kids want to be my partner so they'll win. Even though I have a partner, I usually end up doing most of the work myself! This year, I decided things were going to be different.

Stop   Think   Write

CAUSE AND EFFECT

Why is Josie popular once a year?

_____

_____

_____

I thought of an **elegant** solution to my problem: I would ask Max to be my partner. He's the second smartest kid in class, even though he clowns around a lot. If we did the project together, I knew we would win, and we wouldn't have to compete with each other!

This morning, our teacher announced the date of this year's fair. Right after lunch, I went up to Max. "Would you be my science fair partner?" I asked.

Max looked surprised. "Why me?" he asked.

"Together we can plan a great project," I said. "Neither of us will end up doing all the work!"

"I hear you!" Max said. He knew all about picking a partner who didn't help much. "It's a deal!" he said. "Together we'll create an amazing winning project!"

Stop   Think   Write

CONCLUSIONS AND GENERALIZATIONS

What two words would you use to describe Josie? Explain, using story details.

_____

_____

_____

Max is into space stuff, so he suggested we do something about stars. "The bright city lights make it hard to see the stars!" I reminded him.

I suggested we make a volcano and measure lava flow. "No way," Max said. "That would be too complex and too expensive. We'd need to make volcano models and find a way to simulate lava. We'd have to run hundreds of tests, as well."

Max looked thoughtful. "Let's test which plants make the best natural dyes . . . it would be a project to DYE for!" he laughed.

"Good idea!" I said, glad that I'd picked Max. He was silly sometimes, but he had great ideas. "All we need are plants, a pot, and something to dye!"

The next day, my mom took us shopping. At the market, we bought carrots, lettuce, celery, blueberries, and beets. At a fabric shop, we found white cotton on sale. "We can use this to test the dyes," Max said.

Stop   Think   Write

Which story details suggest that Max and Josie will make good science fair partners?

_____

_____

_____

We spent the next week doing research. We read the basic **principle** for making dyes. Mostly, it's boiling the plants in water. "I like to cook," I said. "Why don't I be in charge of making the dyes? You can be in charge of dyeing the cloth."

Max agreed. So I tested how long to cook the fruits and vegetables, and at what temperatures.

On Saturday, Max came over. I cooked the carrots, and then Max dipped in the cloth. The carrots didn't really color the fabric. We took photos to show our process and also what didn't work.

Next, we tried lettuce and celery, but they were no good either. Then we did blueberries. They were great! The cotton turned blue. Then we tried beets. Great! The cotton turned a bright pinkish red.

Stop   Think   Write

VOCABULARY

What other word could the author have used that means the same as principle?

_____

_____

_____

We needed to try one more plant, and Max suggested bright green leaves from one of Mom's plants. She carefully cut off a few leaves for us. After a few hours of cooking them, I'd made yellow dye!

The next day, Max said, "You know, we should dye things more interesting than bits of cotton!"

I thought that was a great idea. Max donated a white shirt, and we decided it should be dyed blue. The only white thing I had was my stuffed bear. "That bear would look awesome in yellow!" Max said.

At first, I was **reluctant**, but finally I agreed. "So, now what should we make bright red?" I asked.

"I've got a great idea for that," Max said with a smile. "Don't worry. It'll be great. You'll see it at the fair."

Stop   Think   Write

CONCLUSIONS AND GENERALIZATIONS

Why do you think Josie finally agrees to dye her stuffed bear?

_____

_____

_____

On the day of the fair, we set up our display. It was a warm day, but Max was wearing his winter hat. "I overslept and my hair is a mess," he explained.

We hung a sign over our display: WHICH PLANTS DYE BEST? We put up photos of our process. We had the bits of cotton with no results from carrots, lettuce, and celery. We had the colored cotton bits, too. We placed the specimens under their pictures. Finally, we put out the real things we'd dyed. Max's shirt was a perfect blue and my bear had lovely yellow fur. Still, it was obvious that something was missing!

"Where's whatever you dyed red ?" I asked.

"You'll see it soon enough," Max laughed.

"I take competitions seriously, Max," I said.

"So do I, Josie," he replied. "You have to learn to relax and have a little fun!"

Just then, the judges came to our display.

Stop Think Write

What are the **specimens** that Max and Josie place in their display?

_____

_____

_____

"Why is there no red item?" asked one judge. "Your report indicates that you used beets."

"We did," I replied. I stared at Max, waiting for him to answer the judge.

Suddenly, Max ripped off his hat. He had bright red hair! "Ta-da!" he sang. "I've been DYEING to show off my hair all day!"

All the judges laughed. I laughed, too. Max may have done things differently, but he made our project special. He also taught me to have more fun!

Thanks to Max, winning was a lot more fun this year! (We won first prize, of course.)

Stop   Think   Write

CAUSE AND EFFECT

Why do the judges laugh?

_____

_____

_____

Look Back and Respond

1 Why does Josie ask Max to be her partner?

_____

_____

_____

Hint

For a clue, see page 75.

2 Why do you think Josie and Max do so much research before they start making and testing their dyes?

_____

_____

_____

Hint

For clues, see page 77.

3 Tell why Josie and Max are careful to include in their display all the cotton bits from their tests on plant dyes.

_____

_____

_____

Hint

Think about how scientists test their ideas and explain the results.

4 How does working together on the project help both Josie and Max?

_____

_____

_____

Hint

Think about how they work together.

Be a Reading Detective!

Return to

Tripping Over the
Lunch Lady
and Other School Stories

Avi
Angela Johnson
David Lubar
James Proimos
David Rice
Susan Shreve
Terry Trueman
Rachel Vail
Lee Wardlaw
Sarah Weeks

edited by Nancy E. Mercado

"Science Friction"
Student Book pp. 223–235

1 **Which sentence is the best generalization from "Science Friction"?**

☐ People who seem very different can become good friends.

☐ Amanda and Ellen have more in common than they realize.

☐ People who don't like carrots may try to hide them in your room.

Prove It! What evidence in the story supports your answer?
Check the boxes. ☑ Make notes.

Evidence	Notes
☐ what the characters say and do at first	
☐ what the characters say and do at the end of the story	
☐	

Write About It!

CONCLUSIONS AND GENERALIZATIONS

Answer question 1 using evidence from the text.

_____

_____

_____

_____

_____

_____

_____

2 **Amanda thinks that Ellen always has to be Ms. Perfect.**
What is Ellen really like?

☐ She hates cleaning up.

☐ She has to be very organized to get good grades.

☐ She worries about losing things.

☐ other _____

Prove It! What evidence in the story supports your answer?
Check the boxes. ☑   Make notes.

Evidence	Notes
☐ Ellen's words	
☐ Ellen's actions	
☐	

Write About It!

UNDERSTANDING CHARACTERS

Answer question 2 using evidence from the text.

_____

_____

_____

_____

_____

_____

_____

**defy
permeated
rudimentary
sparsely
venture**

WORLD WAR II

in the Pacific

During World War II, many battles were fought on islands in the Pacific Ocean. Japanese soldiers controlled many of the islands. The United States and its allies had to defeat the Japanese in the Pacific if they hoped to win the war.

A culture of pride and obedience permeated the Japanese army. The Japanese were disciplined fighters. Most would never defy their commanders. They were trained to carry out orders without question. They would not stop fighting without an order to do so. This made the Japanese a very fierce enemy.

Many of the islands in the Pacific were sparsely populated. There were often no roads and no towns. Living conditions were rudimentary, with just basic shelter and simple food. Japanese soldiers often hid in the dense jungle. American soldiers had to venture into the jungle to look for the enemy. Capturing each island was a difficult challenge for the Americans and their allies.

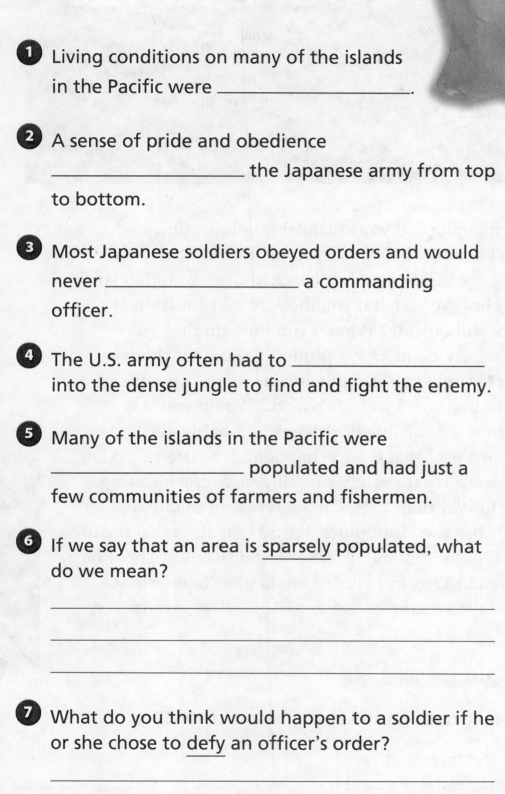

1. Living conditions on many of the islands in the Pacific were _____.

2. A sense of pride and obedience _____ the Japanese army from top to bottom.

3. Most Japanese soldiers obeyed orders and would never _____ a commanding officer.

4. The U.S. army often had to _____ into the dense jungle to find and fight the enemy.

5. Many of the islands in the Pacific were _____ populated and had just a few communities of farmers and fishermen.

6. If we say that an area is sparsely populated, what do we mean?

   _____

   _____

   _____

7. What do you think would happen to a soldier if he or she chose to defy an officer's order?

   _____

   _____

   _____

Hiroo Onoda
The Forgotten Soldier

by Mia Lewis

Imagine that you are outside at lunchtime and don't hear the bell. Once you see that everyone else has gone inside, you'd run back to class, wouldn't you?

However, what if you thought all your friends were still outside? What if you thought they were hiding, trying to *trick* you into thinking lunch was over? Would you stay outside just to defy them and prove their trick wouldn't work? Would you stay outside for, say, an entire week? Probably not.

In a way, that is what happened to Hiroo Onoda. He was a Japanese army intelligence officer during World War II. In 1944, Onoda was sent to Lubang Island, in the Philippines. World War II was raging in the Philippines and on other Pacific islands. The war ended in 1945, but Hiroo Onoda didn't know that. He stayed on the island until he finally surrendered, thirty years later.

Stop Think Write

CAUSE AND EFFECT

Why did Hiroo Onoda go to Lubang Island in 1944?

_____

_____

_____

Following Orders

When Onoda arrived on Lubang Island, it was controlled by the Japanese. Onoda's task was to do everything in his power to stop American forces from taking over the island. Even if he could not stop them, Onoda was to fight the Americans any way he could. He was ordered to keep fighting until his Japanese commander came back for him.

Onoda took his orders very seriously. Soon after he arrived on Lubang Island, American forces took control of it. Japanese soldiers retreated into the jungle and hid in this sparsely inhabited area. The soldiers separated into small groups so they would be harder to find. American soldiers captured or killed most of the Japanese soldiers on the island. Before long, Onoda and three other men were the only Japanese soldiers left in hiding.

Stop Think Write

VOCABULARY

Why do you think the jungle was <u>sparsely</u> inhabited?

_____

_____

_____

The War Ends—Or Does It?

Onoda and the three other soldiers lived on the few supplies they had taken with them into the jungle. They ate bananas and coconuts. Sometimes they killed local farm animals for food. With no real shelter or extra clothes, the Japanese men lived a **rudimentary** life.

Sometimes the soldiers would **venture** out to fight the enemy. The Japanese thought the Americans were still the enemy, but they also suspected local residents. Onoda thought that locals might be spies, or enemy troops in disguise. Sometimes the Japanese attacked locals, killed their animals, or burned their crops.

World War II ended in August of 1945. In October, Onoda saw leaflets that said the war was over and that soldiers should come out of hiding. Onoda did not trust the leaflets. He thought they were a trick. He decided to stay well hidden and follow the orders his commander had given him.

Stop Think Write

CAUSE AND EFFECT

Why did the Japanese soldiers attack local people?

_____

_____

_____

Soldiering On

Year after year, Onoda and his men hid in the jungle. In 1949, one of the soldiers in Onoda's group couldn't take living in isolation any longer. He wanted to surrender. He didn't tell the others. He simply left. He made his way out of the jungle and surrendered to the authorities in Lubang.

Onoda worried that the deserter might tell the enemy where they were hiding. He and the two other Japanese men became more careful than ever. They continued to suspect local people of working with the enemy. They carried out more attacks. Lubang officials sent army patrols to fight back. This led to some small battles between Onoda and local troops.

To Onoda, these battles proved the war was still going on. How could it be over when the enemy was still attacking them? Another of Onoda's men was killed in a battle in 1954. Now, just Onoda and one other man remained.

Stop Think Write

CAUSE AND EFFECT

Why was Onoda convinced that the war was not over?

_____

_____

_____

Come Out, Come Out!

While Hiroo Onoda and his men were in hiding, people tried unsuccessfully to persuade them that the war was over. A great many leaflets were dropped from planes or placed where Japanese soldiers might find them. A surrender order from a Japanese general was printed on one of the leaflets. Newspapers announcing the end of the war were left. Notes and photographs from relatives and friends were dropped from planes. Friends and relatives spoke out over loudspeakers.

Onoda and his men carefully read all the leaflets. They considered every piece of material they found. They always found something suspicious and concluded that the leaflets were a clever trick. They had been at war in the jungle for so long that suspicion permeated their lives. They found it very difficult to trust anyone or anything.

Stop   Think   Write

VOCABULARY

What evidence shows that suspicion <u>permeated</u> the lives of Onoda and his men?

_____

_____

_____

The Search for Onoda

Onoda's final companion died in a battle with locals in 1972. He was fifty-one years old, and he had been hiding for twenty-seven years. Onoda was the only remaining Japanese soldier. Even so, he continued to carry out his commander's orders.

By this time, Hiroo Onoda was something of a legend in Japan. Many people had heard of him. In 1974, a young man named Norio Suzuki left Japan for a trip to the Philippines, Burma, Nepal, and other countries. He said he was going to look for Hiroo Onoda. Amazingly, after just a few days on Lubang, Suzuki found Onoda!

Suzuki told Onoda that World War II was over, but Onoda did not believe him. He said that he would take orders only from his commander. Suzuki took photographs of Onoda. The two men agreed on a hiding place for messages. Then Suzuki went back to Japan. He wanted to help bring Onoda home.

Stop Think Write

INFER AND PREDICT

Why do you think Norio Suzuki took pictures of Onoda?

_____

_____

_____

Out of the Jungle

Norio Suzuki showed the photographs of Onoda to Japanese officials. The government located Major Taniguchi, Onoda's commander from thirty years earlier. Taniguchi now sold books for a living. He agreed to help.

Suzuki left a message for Onoda at their agreed hiding place. He also left copies of the photographs he had taken. Onoda had not seen himself during the entire time he had been hiding in the jungle. He was struck by how much his face had changed.

On March 9, 1974, Major Taniguchi arrived and gave Onoda the order to stop fighting. At long last, Onoda had acceptable proof that the war was over. He handed over his gun and surrendered.

After almost thirty years in hiding, Hiroo Onoda came out of the jungle. He went back to Japan where he received a hero's welcome.

Stop Think Write

CAUSE AND EFFECT

Why did Major Taniguchi have to travel to Lubang to speak to Onoda in person?

_____

_____

_____

Look Back and Respond

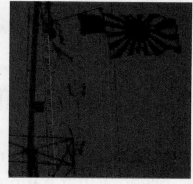

1 Why did Onoda continue to fight for so long?

_____

_____

_____

Hint

For clues, look on pages 85, 88, and 89.

2 Why did one of Onoda's men disobey orders and leave the jungle?

_____

_____

_____

Hint

For clues, look on page 87.

3 Why didn't Onoda and his men believe the leaflets they found?

_____

_____

_____

Hint

For clues, look on page 88.

4 What might have happened if Major Taniguchi had not gone to Lubang Island in 1974?

_____

_____

_____

Hint

Think about what Onoda required before he would stop fighting.

Be a Reading Detective!

Return to

"Kensuke's Kingdom"
Student Book pp. 253–263

1 Michael crosses Kensuke's line and swims in the ocean. What happens as a result?

☐ Kensuke becomes very angry.

☐ Michael is attacked by a jellyfish.

☐ Michael misses his chance to signal the boat.

Prove It! What evidence in the story supports your answer? Check the boxes. ☑ Make notes.

Evidence	Notes
☐ what happens before Michael crosses the line	
☐ what happens after he crosses the line	
☐ Kensuke's reaction when he sees Michael in the ocean	

Write About It!

CAUSE AND EFFECT

Answer question **1** using evidence from the text.

_____

_____

_____

_____

_____

_____

2 As Michael recovers from the jellyfish sting, his feelings change. What does he understand about Kensuke's character now?

☐ Kensuke is a caring and responsible friend.

☐ Kensuke will never let him leave the island.

☐ other _____

Prove It! What evidence in the story supports your answer? Check the boxes. ☑ Make notes.

Evidence	Notes
☐ Kensuke's words	
☐ Kensuke's actions	
☐	

Write About It!

UNDERSTANDING CHARACTERS

Answer question **2** using evidence from the text.

_____

_____

_____

_____

_____

_____

The Inuit

**abundance
cultural
heritage
lore
retains**

In the Arctic tundra, where Inuit communities are located, building materials are scarce. However, there is an **1** _____ of snow. In the past, the Inuit made temporary homes called igloos from hard-packed snow cut into blocks. The domed shape of the igloos helped to hold the heat. Each igloo had a skylight made of freshwater ice. When summer arrived, the igloos melted and the Inuit families moved into tents made of animal skins.

Although Inuit life has changed dramatically over the last century, the Inuit people continue to treasure many of their traditions. Inuit storytelling, mythology, and **2** _____ remain an important part of the **3** _____ life of the Inuit people.

Drumming is an important part of the Inuit **4** _____, too. Drums were traditionally made from driftwood and caribou skin, covered with walrus or seal skin. Drum dancing is used in ceremonies such as marriages, births, and a boy's coming-of-age.

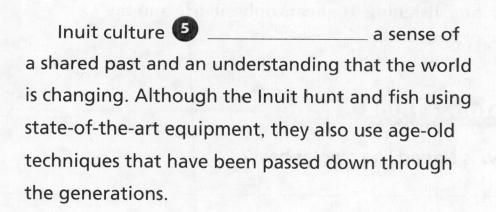

Inuit culture **5** _____ a sense of a shared past and an understanding that the world is changing. Although the Inuit hunt and fish using state-of-the-art equipment, they also use age-old techniques that have been passed down through the generations.

Good Luck, Aputik!

by Dina McClellan

It's winter in the Arctic. In the tiny Inuit village where Nanuq and his family live, it is dark most of the time. The sun peeks out for only a few hours each day. For much of the day, the only light is a faint blue sheen the moon casts over the icy snow.

Nanuq means "polar bear" in the Inuit language, and it suits the boy. He doesn't mind the cold. After the evening meal, he runs out to the wooded area behind his house and follows the familiar trail to the river. He darts through the trees, graceful as a gazelle, careful not to slip on the snow and ice. The river is frozen solid and as smooth as glass. Nanuq sits by the river's edge, breathing in the fresh, clean, northern air. He's waiting, listening. He hears only silence and the howling of the wind.

Stop Think Write

COMPARE AND CONTRAST

How is Nanuq like a polar bear?

_____

_____

_____

Before long, Nanuq hears what he's been waiting for: the *sh-shush* of a dogsled and the soft jingling of bells on the dog collars. It's Aputik's sled coming around the bend!

Nanuq knows that his uncle Aputik is practicing for the Iditarod that will take place the following week. The Iditarod is a race for mushers, who are dogsled racers, and their dog-pulled sleds. The Iditarod starts in southern Alaska and ends 1,100 miles to the northwest. It is very difficult, and only the best mushers compete.

Nanuq wants to be a musher like his uncle, but for now he is content to watch and cheer Aputik from a distance. "Go, Aputik!" Nanuq shouts, jumping up and down and waving his arms. His uncle doesn't hear him. Nanuq watches his sled glide across the snow. Then it vanishes into the dark night as swiftly as it appeared.

Stop Think Write

INFER AND PREDICT

Why do you think Nanuq is not a musher like his uncle?

_____

_____

_____

There is excitement in the village when Nanuq returns. A big celebration in Aputik's honor is about to take place in the snowhouse. People have come from all over by snowmobile and dogsled. There will be drumming, dancing, and singing to wish Aputik good luck. There will also be an **abundance** of food for everyone to eat.

The Inuit have a special way to play drums for dancing and singing. Drumming is part of their **heritage**, and Nanuq's father is an expert. The drum he has brought to the snowhouse used to belong to his father. The drum is large, flat, and round. He plays it by tapping the rim—not the head—on each side. He taps in a steady rhythm that starts out slow and gradually gets faster.

Nanuq's father sways back and forth as he drums. The women of the village, including Nanuq's mother and grandmother, gather around him and sway, too.

Stop Think Write

Write a detail from the text that shows that drumming is part of the <u>heritage</u> of Nanuq's father.

_____

_____

_____

The women sing in a special way called "throat singing." They make sounds deep in their throats. Sometimes the sounds imitate the calls of wolves, foxes, birds, and walruses. Sometimes they are words that tell of real-life experiences. Singing is one way of passing on the tribe's lore from generation to generation.

Tonight the women sing about a team of sled dogs and a brave musher. Their song describes how the musher races for his village and how well he treats his dogs. There is also a young boy in the song who stands by the musher—even on cold, lonely runs by the river.

Everyone understands that the musher in the song is Aputik and that the young boy is Nanuq. Nanuq cannot stop himself from grinning with pleasure. He is proud of his uncle. He is proud of his father, too, because his drumming keeps the rhythm for everyone else.

Stop   Think   Write

COMPARE AND CONTRAST

Write two ways in which the women's song imitates real life.

_____

_____

_____

As the women sing, they form a circle and start to dance. Dancing is a big part of the **cultural** life of the Inuit. No two dances are exactly alike. Like the songs, they are created especially for the occasion. Aputik leaps into the circle and starts stamping the ground to the steady beat of the drums. He whirls and twirls and stomps his feet, never failing to keep the beat. Nanuq is impressed by his uncle's fancy footwork.

The drum dancing and singing go on for hours. Even though it's –30°F (–34.4°C) outside, the snowhouse **retains** warmth. Inside, it is warm and cozy, and the yellow light of a dozen lanterns throws shadows on the walls. Nanuq's father taps faster on the sides of the drum, and the pace of the dance quickens. Then the song ends and the drumming fades out. All Nanuq can hear is the whooshing of the wind outside.

Stop   Think   Write

VOCABULARY

Why is it important that the snowhouse <u>retains</u> warmth?

_____

_____

_____

Suddenly, the silence is broken by wild cheering and the stomping of feet. The people hoot, holler, whoop, yelp, and make animal noises. Cries of "Good luck! Good luck!" can be heard. The women gather around Aputik, clucking and cooing over him, while the men entertain each other with racing lore of the past. Nanuq and his mother squeeze through the crowd to speak to Aputik.

"The song was a special gift for you," says Nanuq's mother. "Carry it in your heart. It will guide you on your journey and keep you safe."

Nanuq looks sad. "I won't be there to cheer you on," he tells his uncle.

The musher smiles and ruffles the boy's hair. "No," he says, "but you will be in my heart. You are a part of my song, and that will bring me good luck."

Nanuq looks into Aputik's dark, shining eyes and knows that what his uncle says is true. Nanuq feels certain that his uncle will win the race, like the brave musher in the song.

Stop   Think   Write

COMPARE AND CONTRAST

According to Nanuq, in what way is Aputik like the musher in the song?

_____

_____

_____

The Iditarod:

The Greatest Race on Earth

* The Iditarod is run on a trail that was originally a mail-supply route.
* The race begins in Anchorage, Alaska. It ends in Nome, Alaska.
* Teams of mushers and dogs complete the race in about 9 to 17 days.

* In 1925, the trail was turned into a lifesaving highway for the children of Nome, Alaska, who were suffering from a deadly disease.
* Unless medicine was delivered, the sick children would die. Teams of mushers and dogs successfully transported the medicine.
* The Iditarod is a tribute to the mushers and dog teams that saved the children of Nome.

* Although sled dogs have been used for thousands of years, the first Iditarod took place in 1973. Thirty-five mushers competed in the race.
* The winner of the first Iditarod completed the race in twenty days. In 2008, the winner finished in just over nine days.

Stop Think Write

COMPARE AND CONTRAST

How has the Iditarod changed between 1973 and today?

_____

_____

_____

Look Back and Respond

1 How is the Arctic climate the same as or different from the climate where you live?

_____

_____

_____

Hint

Compare the setting on page 94 to the climate where you live.

2 Name three things the villagers at the celebration do to honor Aputik.

_____

_____

_____

Hint

For clues, look on pages 96, 97, and 99.

3 How does Nanuq feel about his uncle?

_____

_____

_____

Hint

For clues, look on pages 95, 97, 98, and 99.

4 How does the celebration in the story compare with celebrations that you know?

_____

_____

_____

Hint

Reread the text. Think about celebrations you have attended.

Be a Reading Detective!

Return to

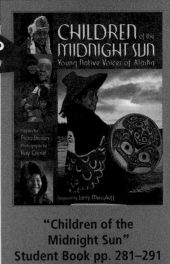

"Children of the Midnight Sun"
Student Book pp. 281–291

1 **Compare Selina and Josh.** In what ways are their lives similar? Choose all correct answers.

☐ They both eat traditional foods, learn about traditional crafts, and do traditional dances.

☐ They both live in small communities in Alaska.

☐ other _____

Prove It! What evidence in the selection supports your answer? Check the boxes. ☑ Make notes.

Evidence	Notes
☐ descriptions of everyday life	
☐ descriptions of locations	
☐ illustrations	

Write About It!

COMPARE AND CONTRAST

Answer question **1** using evidence from the text.

_____

_____

_____

_____

_____

_____

_____

2 **The Haida and the Tlingit both depend on natural resources. What local resources do they use? Choose all correct answers.**

☐ animals that they hunt or fish

☐ trees that they use for boats and crafts

☐ other _____

Prove It! What evidence in the selection supports your answer? Check the boxes. ☑ Make notes.

Evidence	Notes
☐ photos showing fish and trees	
☐ text details about resource use	
☐	

Write About It!

Answer question 2 using evidence from the text.

_____

_____

_____

_____

_____

_____

_____

TARGET VOCABULARY

alleviate
ambled
flared
intense
unrelenting

Fire Emergency

Check the answer.

1 To put out huge flames, fire hoses must shoot a(an) _____ spray of water.

☐ **mild**   ☐ **small**   ☐ **intense**

2 The smoke wouldn't clear, billowing out of the window in a(an) _____ cloud.

☐ **unrelenting**   ☐ **weak**   ☐ **sophisticated**

3 Even though their house was on fire, the odd couple _____ through its hallways, slowly stashing prized possessions.

☐ **flared**   ☐ **ran**   ☐ **ambled**

4 The doctor put a cooling gel on the boy's leg to _____ the pain of the burn.

☐ **hide**   ☐ **alleviate**   ☐ **flare**

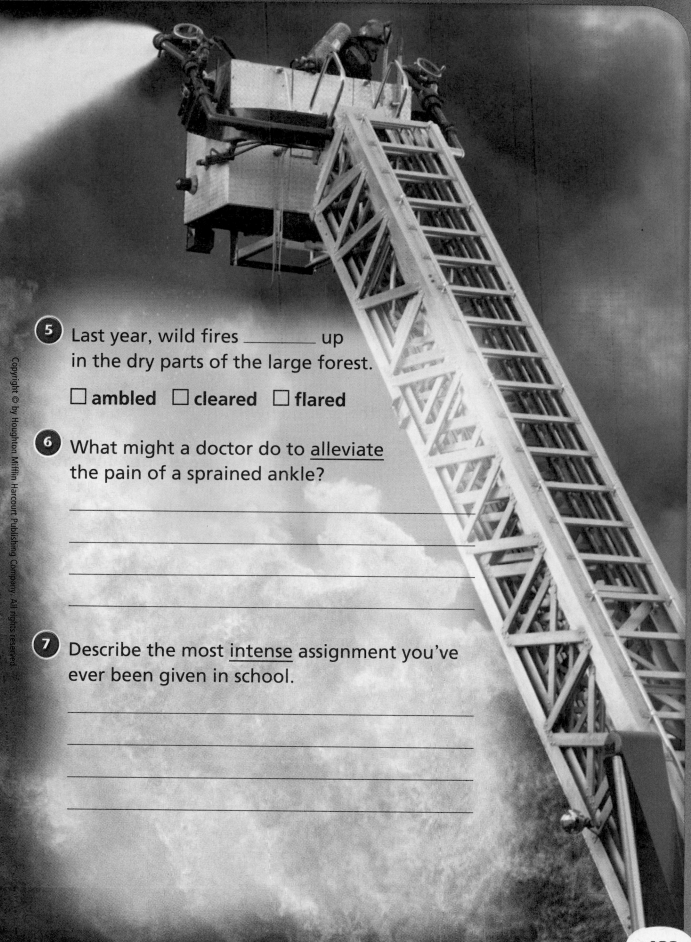

5 Last year, wild fires _____ up in the dry parts of the large forest.

☐ ambled   ☐ cleared   ☐ flared

6 What might a doctor do to <u>alleviate</u> the pain of a sprained ankle?

_____

_____

_____

7 Describe the most <u>intense</u> assignment you've ever been given in school.

_____

_____

_____

_____

The Great Earthquake of 1906

by Justin Shipley

April 18th, 1906, began like any other spring day in the city of San Francisco. A cloudless sky stretched over the bay, and over the city's nearly 400,000 residents. Many were already up, washing and dressing in preparation for the day. Those still fast asleep in their beds would soon be awake.

At 5:12 a.m., the ground beneath the city trembled. Several miles offshore, along the San Andreas Fault, an earthquake had struck. The intense disruption sent shock waves up and down the fault line.

San Francisco experienced the full force of the quake. For a full minute, the earth shook. Objects crashed to the floor as homes were upended, the floors ripped in half by the shifting ground. By the time it was over, the quake had destroyed much of the city, trapping thousands of residents in the rubble of their homes.

Stop Think Write

MAIN IDEA AND DETAILS

Though the city of San Francisco felt its shock waves, where did the earthquake begin?

_____

_____

_____

Though the immediate impact of the earthquake was disastrous, its aftermath was even worse. The quake split many gas lines, and as a result over 30 fires started across the city. Giant fires flared up in buildings. Those who could escape the buildings ran into the streets of the city, only to be met by a blaze. Several fires merged together downtown, creating one huge fire that swept through the city.

To make matters worse, the quake killed the city's Fire Chief, the man whose job it was to make a plan to fight the fires. With its streets littered with flammable material and its Fire Chief dead, San Francisco lit up in flames.

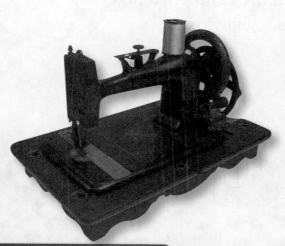

Stop Think Write

SEQUENCE OF EVENTS

Summarize the events that left San Francisco in a terrible emergency.

_____

_____

_____

Wasting no time, the firefighters of San Francisco leapt into action. The quake had broken many of the city's water mains, leaving most fire hydrants useless. The city's firefighters now faced the challenge of fighting the fires with limited options for extinguishing the flames.

Without water, the firefighters decided to make a series of firebreaks to slow the spread of the fire. They tried to use the rubble of destroyed buildings to make the firebreaks. They hoped the rubble would create a barrier to keep the fire from growing.

Stop Think Write

Why did the firefighters decide to make firebreaks?

_____

_____

_____

In order to stop the **unrelenting** flames, the firefighters needed to create more rubble. They decided to demolish partially destroyed buildings with dynamite. The city's acting Fire Chief sent an urgent request for dynamite to an army post just outside the city. The army responded immediately, sending troops and explosives from nearby Angel Island into San Francisco.

Firefighters and soldiers began blowing up buildings across the city. Unfortunately, most of the workers were untrained in the use of explosives. As they exploded, many buildings caught on fire themselves. This did not **alleviate** the spread of the fire. Instead, the dynamite only helped spread the flames further across the city.

Stop Think Write

SEQUENCE OF EVENTS

What happened after the explosives were used?

_____

_____

_____

As their firebreaks failed, the firefighters and troops faced a new problem—panicked citizens. After discovering that insurance would cover damage only by fire and not by the earthquake, some property owners set fire to their own property in order to claim insurance. Shopkeepers whose storefronts had been torn apart by the earthquake started small fires within their stores, lighting curtains and igniting stoves in an effort to make sure they could collect insurance money.

Even as the fires continued to spread, looters began rummaging through the wreckage for valuables. Thieves tore through damaged homes trying to find jewelry and other valuable items. The looting and crime became such a problem that armed troops were sent into the city. The United States Army ordered the troops to shoot any person found looting. Many people were arrested, and order was eventually restored.

Stop   Think   Write

CAUSE AND EFFECT

Why did some property owners in San Francisco set their own property on fire?

_____

_____

_____

The fires continued to rage for four days. When they finally subsided, they had taken an awful toll on the city. Modern researchers estimate that the great fire of 1906 killed nearly 3,000 people, destroyed over 25,000 buildings, and left nearly half of San Francisco's population homeless.

For weeks after the fire, displaced citizens ambled through the streets of the city in a daze, trying to find lost possessions. Former residents set up tents in San Francisco's parks. Many of these shantytowns were still operational nearly two years after the earthquake. The effects of the quake and the fire would be felt for a long time to come.

Stop   Think   Write

VOCABULARY

Besides seeking lost possessions, why else might displaced citizens have <u>ambled</u> through the city?

_____

_____

_____

Plans to rebuild San Francisco began almost immediately after the fires died. Local and national people worked to rebuild the city, paving wider streets, building a subway, and fixing famous buildings.

By 1915, San Francisco had been completely restored. Since then, the city has remembered the disaster every year by holding a gathering at Lotta's Fountain, a famous landmark in the heart of San Francisco. To this day, the earthquake remains a reminder of the awesome power of nature.

Stop Think Write

SUMMARIZE

In what ways did nature change San Francisco?

_____

_____

_____

Look Back and Respond

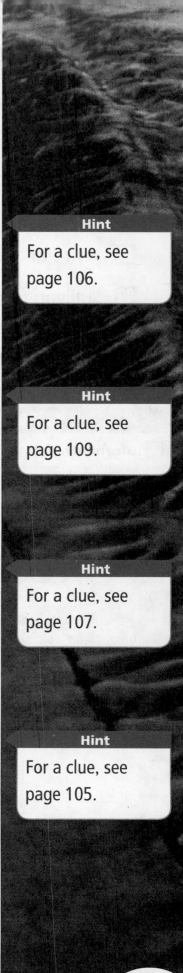

1 Why did firefighters try to contain the fire with firebreaks?

_____

_____

_____

Hint

For a clue, see page 106.

2 How did people act in the weeks after the earthquake?

_____

_____

_____

Hint

For a clue, see page 109.

3 Why did the acting Fire Chief ask the army for help?

_____

_____

_____

Hint

For a clue, see page 107.

4 How did the fires first start?

_____

_____

_____

Hint

For a clue, see page 105.

Be a Reading Detective!

Return to

JIM MURPHY

"The Great Fire"
Student Book pp. 313–325

1 **Which event happened first?**

☐ A fire broke out at the O'Learys' barn.

☐ A fire on October 7 destroyed four blocks.

☐ Sullivan rescued a calf.

Prove It! What evidence in the selection supports your answer?
Check the boxes. ☑ Make notes.

Evidence	Notes
☐ information about dates	
☐ information about the start of the fire	
☐	

Write About It!

SEQUENCE OF EVENTS

Answer question **1** using evidence from the text.

_____

_____

_____

_____

_____

_____

_____

2 **Why did the Chicago fire spread so quickly?**

☐ things people did

☐ things caused by nature

☐ both of the above

Prove It! What evidence in the selection supports your answer? Check the boxes. ☑ Make notes.

Evidence	Notes
☐ the buildings	
☐ the weather	
☐ what people stored	
☐	

Write About It!

CAUSE AND EFFECT

Answer question 2 using evidence from the text.

_____

_____

_____

_____

_____

_____

Hot-Air Balloons

✓ TARGET VOCABULARY

engulf
falter
frail
relishing
undulating

1 Even a brave person would **falter** at the thought of circling the globe in a hot-air balloon. Yet, for over a century, people have overcome their hesitations and fears and tried to do just that.

What kind of journey might make you <u>falter</u>?

_____

_____

_____

2 In 1783, the Montgolfier brothers built a balloon out of thin silk, paper, and a basket. Onlookers must have thought they were foolish to put their faith in such a **frail** craft. However, the balloon was able to fly over a mile.

Name an object that looks <u>frail</u> but is surprisingly strong. Explain.

_____

_____

_____

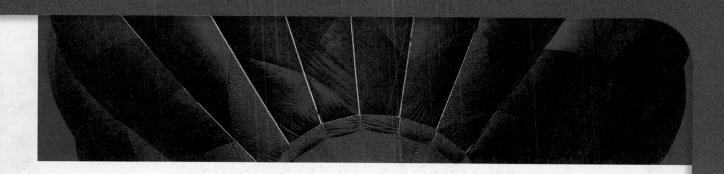

3 The crowd watched the balloon **undulating** in the breeze. It moved slowly up and down with a gentle motion.

What things can make an undulating motion?

_____

_____

_____

4 As a balloon rises higher, clouds may **engulf** it. Higher up, the balloon may break through the clouds and into the sunshine.

What is a synonym for engulf?

_____

5 **Relishing** the freedom of floating in the air, some people make frequent balloon trips. People can even take short balloon trips at fairgrounds.

What is an activity that you have been relishing this year?

_____

_____

_____

High Fliers
by Carol Alexander

High in the snowy mountains of Switzerland, two men watched the skies. Their craft, the *Breitling Orbiter III*, swayed in the wind. The weather had been uncertain. At last, the ground crew gave them the okay.

Bertrand Piccard turned to his copilot, Brian Jones. "I think it's time," he said.

News reporters circled the *Breitling Orbiter*. Excitement ran high in the crowd. "If this flight is successful, Piccard and Jones will have made history!" a reporter exclaimed into her microphone. "These two men will attempt to circle the globe in a balloon! People have tried to do this for years, ever since Jules Verne wrote about the idea in his novel *Around the World in Eighty Days*."

Stop   Think   Write

STORY STRUCTURE

What event is the crowd waiting for?

_____

_____

_____

A second reporter added, "That's right. All previous attempts have failed, but maybe this balloon will succeed. Look at it—it's about as tall as the Statue of Liberty! The outer layers of the balloon engulf another envelope inside. That one contains helium, which is lighter than air. Surrounding the helium envelope is regular air. The pilots will heat the air to make the balloon ascend."

"Didn't Piccard try before?" a man in the crowd asked.

"Yes, he's actually tried twice before. The third time might be the charm," said the reporter.

The trip would not be easy, but Bertrand Piccard had adventure in his blood. His grandfather had been a hot-air balloonist. Piccard's father had explored the depths of the ocean. They were a family of adventurers.

Stop   Think   Write

AUTHOR'S PURPOSE

Why does the author mention earlier, unsuccessful flights?

_____

_____

_____

Piccard was not one to **falter**. He and Jones would put their trust in the winds—and in the ground crew. The ground crew was an important part of the team. They would advise Piccard and Jones of weather conditions and make sure the flight path was cleared with different countries around the world.

The takeoff was smooth, the balloon **undulating** in the wind. The men headed south toward Morocco. They could not steer, but they could make the balloon go up or down by using propane burners to heat the gas. They had to be careful not to use too much propane, or they wouldn't have enough to finish the trip.

The balloon flew over storm clouds and mountaintops. After reaching Morocco, the balloon went east across the Sahara Desert. Then the men ran into their first problem. The country of Yemen refused to give the balloonists permission to fly over its air space. Piccard and Jones might have to land.

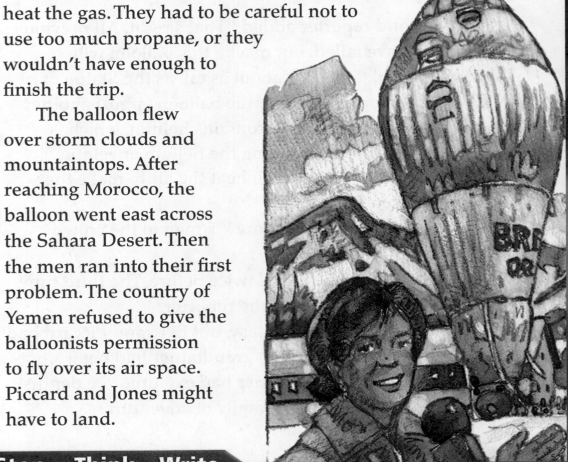

Stop Think Write

VOCABULARY

What does the author mean when she writes that "Piccard was not one to <u>falter</u>"?

_____

_____

_____

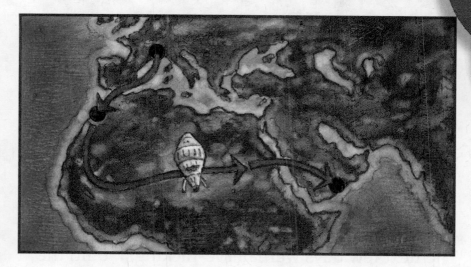

At that moment, the men in the air realized how **frail** their craft really was. The armed forces of Yemen might attempt to shoot them down. However, their luck held out, and they crossed the region safely.

Another balloon that had set out on a round-the-world trip two weeks earlier had not been so lucky. It had been forced to land in the ocean due to ice build-up on its surface. When they heard from the ground crew about the forced landing, Piccard and Jones were concerned. Although the other balloon was no longer their competition, the pilots were their friends. They were glad to find out that the pilots were safely rescued.

There was more trouble for the *Breitling Orbiter* as it neared China. Chinese air traffic control didn't want the balloon to fly over Chinese air space.

Piccard cried, "We spent over a year getting the approval for this part of our trip!"

Stop Think Write

VOCABULARY

What made Piccard and Jones realize that their balloon was <u>frail</u>?

_____

_____

_____

The next few days were nerve-racking. Would the Chinese stop the balloon? Not everyone on the ground understood how balloons fly. They couldn't be steered like airplanes. Balloon pilots could not predict an exact course. The language problem made things difficult, too.

A week later, the balloon cleared the Chinese border. Next, they would cross the Pacific Ocean. That part of the trip would be longer than the whole way they had come so far. It could be very dangerous because there was no place to land.

Piccard wrote in his diary, "This is exactly my definition of adventure.... You have to dig inside yourself to find the courage and resources to deal with what may lie ahead."

The men soon had a decision to make. The clouds to the north could kill them because the temperature might disable the balloon. Going south would add a thousand miles to the trip. Would they have enough fuel?

Stop Think Write

STORY STRUCTURE

Why might the trip across the Pacific Ocean be dangerous?

_____

_____

_____

As the balloon headed south, the weather turned harsh. The men rose high above the clouds to escape it. The air in the cabin grew freezing. The men put on all the clothing they had. They slept in three sleeping bags. It grew very difficult to breathe. The ground crew told them to use oxygen, which helped.

At last, the Pacific Ocean was behind the men. Now Piccard and Jones had to face another problem. The balloon was running out of fuel. Here they were on the final leg of the trip. Did they dare try to fly over the Atlantic Ocean? Should they try landing or go for it?

Piccard said, "The only way to fail is to quit, and we're not going to quit!"

On the ground, the Swiss news reporters followed the story closely. Would Piccard and Jones make history? Or would they be forced to give up?

Stop Think Write

CAUSE AND EFFECT

Why did Piccard and Jones have to consider whether or not to cross the Atlantic Ocean?

_____

_____

_____

The Atlantic crossing was successful. The balloon was heading over the African continent. Then the radio stopped working. After three weeks of bad food, thin air, and close quarters, the pilots had lost touch with the ground crew.

Miles over the Earth, the men did not even realize they had reached their goal. They had circled the globe. Piccard found a strange beauty in the desert crossing. Relishing the view, he told Jones, "Looking over the desert makes up for all of it. To me, the star-filled sky and the sand below are truly magical."

At last, the men landed in the desert of Egypt. They waited in unending miles of sand for the rescue team. An excited reporter asked them, "Did you take anything along for good luck?"

Brian Jones told the reporter, "Yes, we did. We had a book that once belonged to Jules Verne."

Stop   Think   Write

STORY STRUCTURE

Why didn't Piccard and Jones realize they had completed their trip around the globe?

_____

_____

_____

Look Back and Respond

1 How would you describe Bertrand Piccard?

_____

_____

_____

Hint

For clues, see pages 115, 116, 118, and 119.

2 How does the setting change through the story?

_____

_____

_____

Hint

Clues you can use are on almost every page.

3 What danger did the pilots run into as they crossed Yemen?

_____

_____

_____

Hint

For a clue, see pages 116 and 117.

4 Why did Piccard and Jones take along a book that had belonged to Jules Verne?

_____

_____

_____

Hint

For clues, see pages 114 and 120.

Be a Reading Detective!

Return to

"Airborn"
Student Book pp. 345–359

1 **When does the story take place?**

☐ in the middle of the day

☐ in the late afternoon

☐ at night

Prove It! What evidence in the story supports your answer?
Check the boxes. ☑ Make notes.

Evidence	Notes
☐ illustrations	
☐ what Matt does at the end	
☐ descriptions in the text	
☐	

Write About It!

STORY STRUCTURE

Answer question ❶ using evidence from the text.

_____

_____

_____

_____

_____

_____

_____

2 **What is most important to Matt after the rescue?**

☐ He knows he is fearless.

☐ The captain compliments him.

☐ The captain tells him his father would be proud.

☐ other _____

Prove It! What evidence in the story supports your answer?
Check the boxes. ☑ Make notes.

Evidence	Notes
☐ what the captain says	
☐ how Matt feels when he is commended	
☐ how Matt feels about what he has to do	
☐	

Write About It!

Answer question ② using evidence from the text.

_____

_____

_____

_____

_____

_____

culmination
expanse
frigid
prime
sacrificed

Polar Exploration

1 In the early 1900s, many explorers traveled to the Arctic. Some tried to reach the North Pole. Reaching the Pole would be the **culmination** of an Arctic explorer's dreams. There could be no higher achievement.

Write a synonym for <u>culmination</u>.

_____

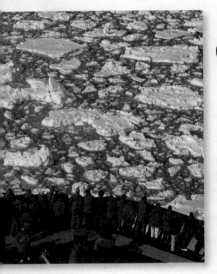

2 The Arctic was a vast **expanse** of cold seas and ice. In the late 1800s and early 1900s, explorers tried to map this huge territory. Some also sailed south to explore the region called Antarctica.

Name and describe an <u>expanse</u> of land in your state or community.

_____

_____

_____

3 Early Arctic explorers faced <mark>frigid</mark> weather. Winter temperatures in the Arctic averaged around -30°F (-34°C). In Antarctica, the climate was even colder.

What is the most frigid weather you have ever experienced? How did it affect you?

_____

_____

_____

4 Polar explorers needed to prepare for the harsh climate at the Poles. They would <mark>prime</mark> themselves by exercising in high altitudes and hiking in cold, snow-covered regions.

How might runners prime themselves for a big race?

_____

_____

_____

5 Early polar explorers <mark>sacrificed</mark> a great deal. Some went into debt to pay for their trips. They suffered pain and hardship in a cold, dark climate. Most explorers felt that the prize of reaching the North or South Pole was worth great hardship.

Tell about a time when you <u>sacrificed</u> something. Why did you make the sacrifice?

_____

_____

_____

The Race to the South Pole

by Duncan Searl

Roald Amundsen couldn't believe the news. The American explorers Robert Peary and Matthew Henson had just reached the North Pole. This was a disaster for Amundsen.

For two years, he had been carefully planning his own voyage to the North Pole. His ship, the *Fram*, was stocked for the Arctic voyage. His crew was ready. He even had sled dogs.

It had taken great effort to prime himself for the trip, but Amundsen saw no reason to go now. He didn't want to be the second person to reach the North Pole. There was no glory in that. There would be no riches either, and that was important. To pay for his voyage, Amundsen had planned to write a book about being the first person to reach the Pole.

Standing on the deck of the *Fram*, the thirty-eight-year-old Norwegian explorer slowly turned. He had been staring north. Now, he gazed southward. "Maybe there is another way," he thought.

Stop   Think   Write

MAIN IDEAS AND DETAILS

Why was Robert Peary's success a disaster for Roald Amundsen?

Change of Plans

The first person to reach the South Pole would enjoy fame and glory, too. Several explorers had tried, but they had all failed. Roald Amundsen made a sudden decision. Instead of sailing to "the top of the world," he would sail to the bottom!

The *Fram* left Oslo, Norway, in June of 1910. The sailors thought they were sailing north to the Arctic. Once they were out at sea, they learned the truth. Their real destination was Antarctica—12,000 miles to the south!

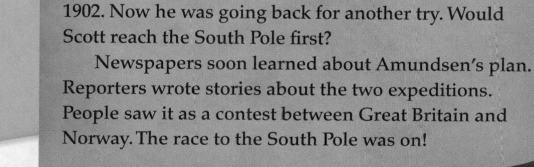

Amundsen had learned that another explorer was sailing to Antarctica, too. Robert Scott of Great Britain had failed to reach the South Pole in 1902. Now he was going back for another try. Would Scott reach the South Pole first?

Newspapers soon learned about Amundsen's plan. Reporters wrote stories about the two expeditions. People saw it as a contest between Great Britain and Norway. The race to the South Pole was on!

Stop Think Write

MAIN IDEAS AND DETAILS

Why was Robert Scott a problem for Roald Amundsen?

_____

_____

_____

Winter in the Antarctic

On January 11, 1911, the *Fram* reached the Ross Ice Shelf in Antarctica. This **expanse** of ice lies 760 miles from the South Pole. The Norwegians built a hut on the ice. They unloaded their supplies and dogs. Only seven men stayed with Amundsen. The others sailed to Argentina before ice could trap the ship.

The long winter began. There would be six months of total darkness. Inside their hut, the explorers wondered what lay ahead. They would be traveling through unmapped territory to reach the South Pole. They didn't know what obstacles they might find.

In August, the sunlight finally returned. In September, however, the temperature was still a **frigid** -63° F (-53°C). Amundsen and his men had to wait another month before it was warm enough to travel.

Robert Scott and his team spent the winter 400 miles to the west of Amundsen. They didn't have to worry about their route. On an earlier trip, British explorers had come within 100 miles of the South Pole. Captain Scott planned to go the same way this time.

Stop   Think   Write

VOCABULARY

Why was <u>frigid</u> weather a problem for the explorers?

_____

_____

_____

Setting Out for the South Pole

On October 20, Roald Amundsen and four companions loaded their dogsleds. Strapping on their skis, they set out. Despite snowy weather, the Norwegians made good progress on the ice shelf. Sometimes, the sled dogs even towed the men and the sleds.

In the distance, however, a problem loomed. The Queen Maud Mountains came into view. These high peaks blocked Amundsen's path, for the South Pole sat on a high plateau on the other side of the mountains.

Captain Scott's party didn't start out until November 3. Their expedition was large, with sixteen men, thirteen sleds, twenty-three dogs, and ten ponies. Scott's group moved slowly. Two of the sleds had motors, but they broke down. The ponies had trouble walking on ice, and they slowed the progress of the dogsleds. To make matters worse, a snowstorm stopped Scott for five days.

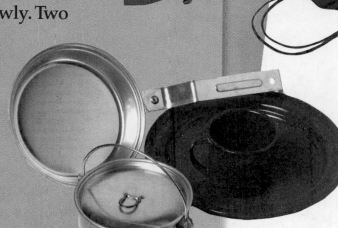

Stop   Think   Write

COMPARE AND CONTRAST

How was Robert Scott's expedition different from Roald Amundsen's?

_____

_____

_____

Rough Going

Near the mountains, Roald Amundsen spotted a long streak of ice. A glacier, 10,000 feet high, had formed between two peaks. Climbing that steep, icy slope was the only way to cross the mountains.

The struggle up the glacier took days. Two teams of dogs were needed to pull each sled. The men had to push the sleds, too. Deep, wide cracks in the ice made the climb dangerous.

At the top of the glacier, the Norwegians buried supplies for their return journey. Then they sacrificed their weakest dogs to provide food. This was sad but necessary for their survival.

To the west, Robert Scott also faced a glacier. Before climbing it, he sacrificed his ponies for food. Then he sent all the dogs and empty sleds back to his base camp.

Scott's glacier wasn't as steep as Amundsen's. However, the climb was exhausting. Without dogs, the men had to drag their heavy sleds. One man fell down a deep hole in the ice. By the time Scott reached the top of the glacier, it was December 25, 1911.

Stop Think Write

Why were dogs and ponies <u>sacrificed</u> by the explorers?

_____

_____

_____

Success!

Once they passed the glacier, Amundsen and his men skied south. Just 250 miles of level land separated them from their goal. Each day, they looked for signs of the British. Was Captain Scott ahead of them?

On December 13, 1911, the explorers were just fifteen miles from the South Pole. The **culmination** of years of planning was near. Amundsen was too excited to sleep. To prepare for reaching the South Pole, he tied a Norwegian flag to his ski pole.

The next day, Amundsen planted that flag at 90° south—the South Pole. For two days, the explorers circled for miles around the spot. They took measurements and observed the sun. They made absolutely sure they were at the right place.

Captain Scott, of course, was behind Amundsen. The British explorers didn't reach the South Pole until January 17, 1912. There they saw the Norwegian flag. "It is a terrible disappointment," Scott wrote.

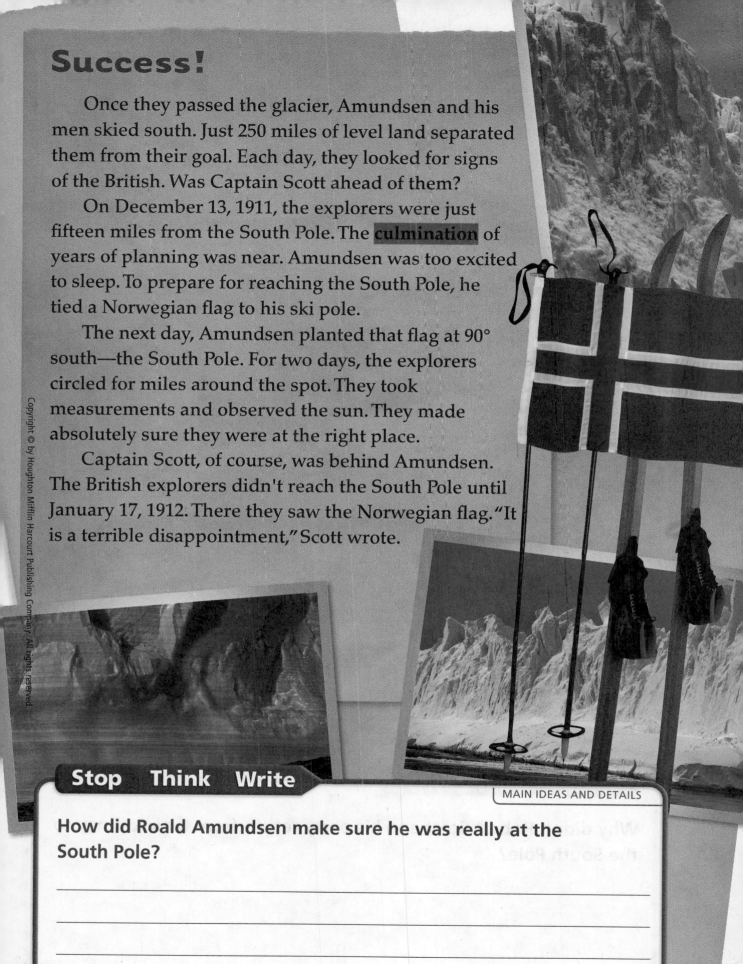

Stop Think Write

MAIN IDEAS AND DETAILS

How did Roald Amundsen make sure he was really at the South Pole?

_____

_____

_____

Homeward Bound

Amundsen's return trip went without a hitch. The weather remained sunny. The dogs helped pull the skiers. Once down the glacier, everyone raced across the ice shelf. The *Fram* was waiting, and on January 25, 1912, the explorers were on board.

Amundsen sailed to South America. There, he published reports about his trip. He later traveled the world giving speeches. He also wrote a best-selling book. Amundsen earned enough money to pay for his expedition and to pay for more adventures, too.

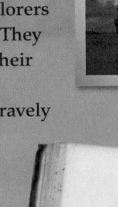

Tragically, Robert Scott never did return from the Antarctic. During his homeward trek, a blizzard struck. By then, the British explorers were exhausted from pulling their sleds. They tried to wait out the storm in a tent, but their food and fuel ran out.

Roald Amundsen and Robert Scott bravely challenged an icy climate and unknown terrain in order to reach the South Pole. Their achievements encouraged others to explore Antarctica. Each year, scientists learn more and more about this important continent.

Stop Think Write

MAIN IDEAS AND DETAILS

Why didn't Robert Scott and his party return from their journey to the South Pole?

_____

_____

_____

Look Back and Respond

1 **In just a few sentences, describe what this text is about.**

_____

_____

_____

Hint

Include only the most important information in your response.

2 **In 1910, Roald Amundsen suddenly decided to go to the South Pole, not the North Pole. What factors influenced him and made the trip possible?**

_____

_____

_____

Hint

For clues, see pages 124 and 125.

3 **Why do you think that Roald Amundsen, not Robert Scott, won the race to the South Pole?**

_____

_____

_____

Hint

For clues, see pages 127, 128, and 129.

4 **What might someone like Roald Amundsen do in today's world? Explain.**

_____

_____

_____

Hint

Think about what kind of person Amundsen was.

Be a Reading Detective!

Return to

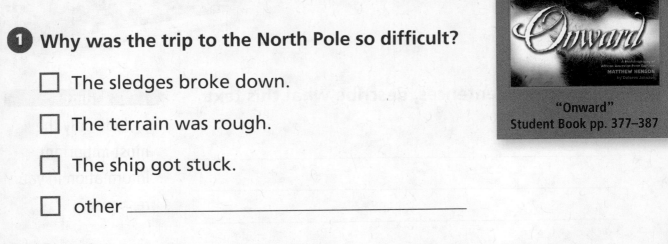

"Onward"
Student Book pp. 377–387

1 Why was the trip to the North Pole so difficult?

☐ The sledges broke down.

☐ The terrain was rough.

☐ The ship got stuck.

☐ other _____

Prove It! What evidence in the selection supports your answer?
Check the boxes. ☑   Make notes.

Evidence	Notes
☐ details about leads and the ice bridge	
☐ the photographs	
☐ the captions	
☐	

Write About It!

MAIN IDEAS AND DETAILS

Answer question **1** using evidence from the text.

_____

_____

_____

_____

_____

_____

_____

2 **Which opinion could you support with evidence from the text?**

☐ Peary could have reached the Pole by himself.

☐ Peary needed Henson's help to reach the Pole.

☐ The Inuit were the most helpful people on the expedition.

Prove It! What evidence in the selection supports your answer? Check the boxes. ☑ Make notes.

Evidence	Notes
☐ events during the journey	
☐ preparation for the journey	
☐ expertise and experience	
☐	

Write About It!

Answer question **2** **using evidence from the text.**

_____

_____

_____

_____

_____

_____

_____

✓ TARGET VOCABULARY

aim
emulate
motive
skeptical
understatement

More Than a Teacher

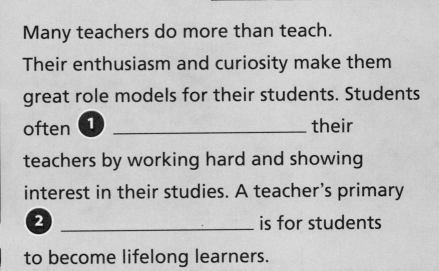

Many teachers do more than teach. Their enthusiasm and curiosity make them great role models for their students. Students often **1** _____ their teachers by working hard and showing interest in their studies. A teacher's primary **2** _____ is for students to become lifelong learners.

Some students are ❸ _____
of their abilities to do well in school. Teachers
might offer a prize to encourage these students
to work extra hard on a project or a test. The
prize gives students a ❹ _____
to work extra hard to do a good job.

One teacher gave a pizza party for the students
who showed the greatest improvement. It
would be an ❺ _____ to
say that the winners were pleased. They were
absolutely thrilled!

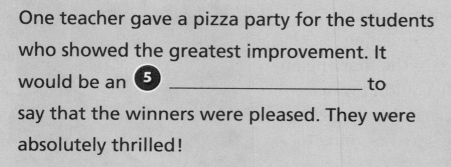

Raúl's Landscape

by Mia Lewis

Bold charcoal lines streaked up the page to a copper-colored sky. Raúl gazed out his bedroom window at the urban landscape. His fingers flew across the page as he added details and highlights to his drawing. Sometimes Raúl tried to emulate the colors and shapes that his art teacher, Mrs. Hernandez, liked to use. Today, however, the style of his sketch was entirely his own.

Darkness was falling, but Raúl kept working. He had a strong motive to finish his drawing. If he turned it in tomorrow, and if it was one of the five best drawings in the school, it would be included in the district art fair.

Raúl added a few finishing touches and then gave the drawing an appraising look. He couldn't wait to hear what Mrs. Hernandez thought of it. He had a feeling she was going to like it.

Stop Think Write

VOCABULARY

In what ways might Raúl **emulate** his art teacher?

_____

_____

_____

"Raúl, are you done with your homework?" his mother called. "It's time for the twins to go to bed."

Raúl's mom came into the room with a pajama-clad boy on each hip. Raúl called the twins "double trouble," because they were always into something. At the moment, they were too sleepy to cause trouble. Raúl and his mother tucked José and Luis into their cribs. Then Raúl finished his homework and went to bed.

The next morning, Raúl thought about how to get his drawing safely to school without folding or wrinkling it.

"What about the cardboard tube from the wrapping paper?" suggested his mom. "It's in my room."

Raúl checked that the twins were occupied before dashing into his mother's room to retrieve the roll. When he returned, Raúl's eyes bulged. The twins had his drawing and were scribbling all over it.

Stop　Think　Write

STORY STRUCTURE

What problem have the twins created for Raúl?

_____

_____

_____

"Oh, no!" Raúl yelled. He snatched his drawing and the charcoal pencils from the twins. "Mom! They've ruined my drawing! What a disaster!"

"Calm down," his mom said gently. "Did you make it for a special assignment? I'm sure your teacher will understand if you explain what happened."

"Special assignment?" said Raúl. "That's an **understatement**! That drawing was my only chance to be chosen for the district art fair. If the drawing isn't submitted to the district art fair, then I'll miss out on the state art fair, too!"

His mom said that she was sure everything would be all right once he explained what had happened to Mrs. Hernandez. Raúl wasn't so sure. He was subdued on the way to school. His friends had made drawings, but to them, the art fair was simply a lark. For Raúl, the art fair was like the World Series. He was at the top of the league—and ready for the championship game!

Stop Think Write

MAKE INFERENCES

What does the author mean when she says Raúl was "at the top of the league—and ready for the championship game"?

_____

_____

_____

136

As soon as he got to school, Raúl went to find Mrs. Hernandez. He unrolled the ruined drawing and told her what had happened. Mrs. Hernandez seemed as crestfallen as Raúl.

"Raúl," she said, "haven't I always taught you to work through problems? You've learned not to give up on a drawing until you get it right, and I don't want you to give up on this, either. You're a talented artist, and my **aim** is to find a way for you to enter the district art fair."

"I believe there's a way you can still enter the contest," Mrs. Hernandez continued. "Mr. Wang, the principal, and I will choose the five best drawings from each grade after school. We will be bringing those winners to the Art Institute of Chicago, where they will be displayed with the entries from other schools. If you can bring us another landscape by the time we start reviewing our entries, we will be able to consider your drawing, too."

Stop   Think   Write

VOCABULARY

Do you think Raúl shares the same <u>aim</u> as Mrs. Hernandez? Explain.

_____

_____

_____

Mrs. Hernandez had always encouraged Raúl, and he had learned a lot since she had become his teacher. It made him feel good to know that she believed in him, but he was still skeptical. How could he possibly finish another drawing during the school day?

Raúl slaved over his drawing every spare minute that day. Mrs. Hernandez set up a table for him, and he worked there while he nibbled on his lunch and during study hall. Mrs. Hernandez even arranged for him to skip gym class so that he could spend more time on his drawing. (He promised to make up the class the next day.) His landscape was taking shape again, but slowly!

Too soon, the last bell of the day rang. Raúl ran to the art room and kept drawing. Then Mr. Wang showed up, and it was time for the judging. Raúl's landscape was so close to being done that it hurt to think about it! Raúl turned away from the teachers and wiped his eyes.

Stop Think Write

THEME

How does Mrs. Hernandez help Raúl work through his problem?

_____

_____

_____

Mr. Wang and Mrs. Hernandez looked at all the drawings. They spoke quietly together before returning to the table where Raúl stood.

"Even though your landscape is not quite done, it's still one of the best drawings here," said Mr. Wang. "Do you think you can complete it and bring it to the Art Institute by nine o'clock tonight?"

Raúl was ecstatic. "I'm not about to give up now!" he said. "I'll do my best to get it there on time." He thanked the teachers, rolled up his picture, and headed home as fast as he could. He ran to his room and worked without stopping until the drawing was finished.

Now, he and his dad just had to make it to the Art Institute before nine o'clock. It was already after eight. Raúl's mom was at class. That meant two cranky and sleepy little boys had to come with them across town.

Stop Think Write

Why do Mr. Wang and Mrs. Hernandez ask Raúl to bring his finished drawing to the Art Institute by nine o'clock?

_____

_____

_____

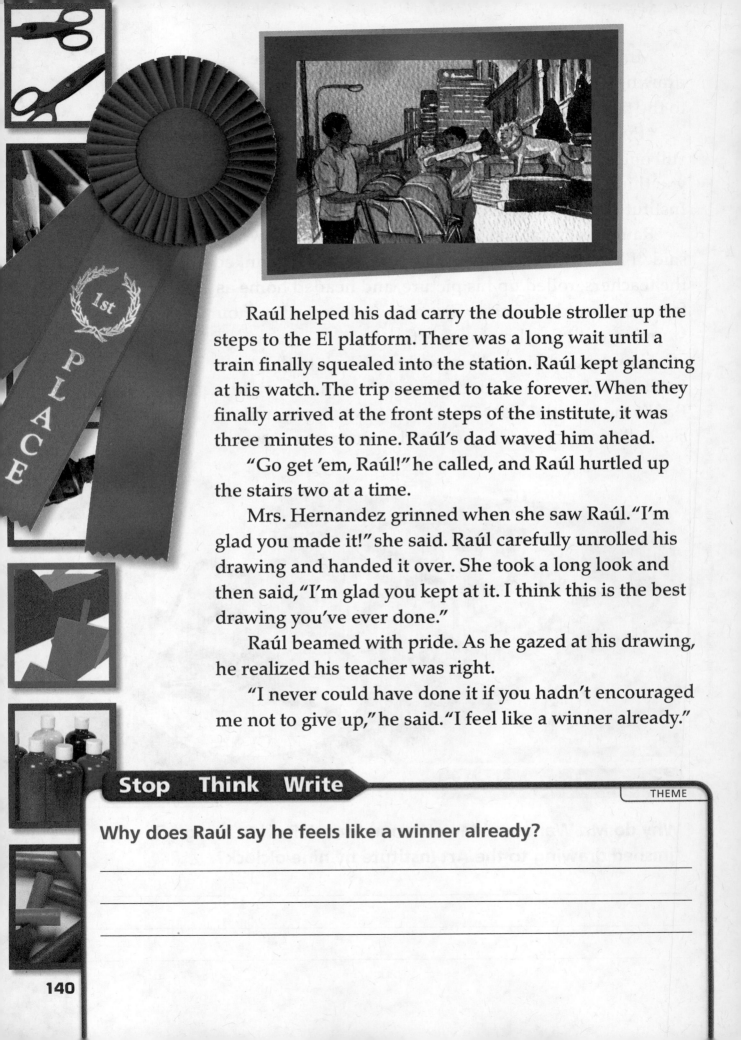

Raúl helped his dad carry the double stroller up the steps to the El platform. There was a long wait until a train finally squealed into the station. Raúl kept glancing at his watch. The trip seemed to take forever. When they finally arrived at the front steps of the institute, it was three minutes to nine. Raúl's dad waved him ahead.

"Go get 'em, Raúl!" he called, and Raúl hurtled up the stairs two at a time.

Mrs. Hernandez grinned when she saw Raúl. "I'm glad you made it!" she said. Raúl carefully unrolled his drawing and handed it over. She took a long look and then said, "I'm glad you kept at it. I think this is the best drawing you've ever done."

Raúl beamed with pride. As he gazed at his drawing, he realized his teacher was right.

"I never could have done it if you hadn't encouraged me not to give up," he said. "I feel like a winner already."

Stop Think Write

THEME

Why does Raúl say he feels like a winner already?

_____

_____

_____

Look Back and Respond

1 What is the theme, or main lesson, that the author expresses in this story? Explain.

_____
_____
_____

Hint

For clues, see pages 137 and 140. What advice does Mrs. Hernandez give Raúl?

2 How does the author show that Raúl is serious about his art?

_____
_____
_____

Hint

Clues are on almost every page.

3 Name some different ways that the adults help Raúl succeed.

_____
_____
_____

Hint

For clues, see pages 137, 138, 139, and 140.

4 Why do you think the author does not name the prize winners of the district art fair?

_____
_____
_____

Hint

Think of how events should build to give the theme. Would the names be helpful?

141

Be a Reading Detective!

Return to

"Any Small Goodness"
Student Book pp. 407–417

1 What is the theme, or message, of "Any Small Goodness"?

☐ Help those who need it the most.

☐ Try hard, and you will become the best.

☐ Family is the most important thing.

☐ other _____

Prove It! What evidence in the story supports your answer? Check the boxes. ☑ Make notes.

Evidence	Notes
☐ Coach Tree's actions and his tiny salary	
☐ Arturo's thoughts about Coach Tree	
☐ Arturo's thoughts about his future	

Write About It!

THEME

Answer question **1** using evidence from the text.

_____

_____

_____

_____

_____

_____

_____

2 **What kind of person is Coach Tree?**

☐ He is a star who thinks he is too important to pay attention to anyone else.

☐ He is a kind person with a good sense of humor.

☐ other _____

Prove It! What evidence in the story supports your answer? Check the boxes. ☑ Make notes.

Evidence	Notes
☐ what Coach Tree says	
☐ what the players say about Coach Tree	
☐ what Coach Tree does for José	
☐	

Write About It!

UNDERSTANDING CHARACTERS

Answer question **2** using evidence from the text.

_____

_____

_____

_____

_____

_____

_____

TARGET VOCABULARY

ascent
hovering
lunar
option
perilous

Driving on the Moon

1 Some Apollo missions carried **lunar** rovers. These vehicles helped astronauts explore bigger areas of the Moon's surface.

If you could make a <u>lunar</u> vehicle, what would you include in your design?

_____

_____

_____

A lunar rover

2 A rover could carry two astronauts and travel uphill, downhill, and on flat surfaces. Traveling uphill required the most power, so the rover's four electric motors worked especially hard during an **ascent**.

Think about a time you walked over a hill or up a mountain. What was the <u>ascent</u> like?

_____

_____

_____

3 Driving a lunar rover on the Moon was **perilous**. If the rover broke down, the astronauts had to hope they could repair it themselves. They relied on their space suits to protect them from the Moon's atmosphere, which is cold and has no oxygen.

What do you think is the most perilous part of a space trip?

_____

_____

_____

4 Modern lunar rovers can travel more than fifty miles. Astronauts have the **option** to travel far from where they land, but they might choose to stay close to their spacecraft. If the lunar rover breaks down, they would not have to walk far to get back.

Tell about a time when you had to decide between a few possible choices. Which option did you choose?

_____

_____

_____

5 Astronauts on the Moon could see Earth. At times, our planet looked as if it were **hovering** over the lunar horizon.

What is the difference between hovering over the ground and flying back and forth in the air?

_____

_____

_____

The Lunar Module
Engineered to Serve
by John Berry

Project Apollo was a series of space flights carried out in the 1960s and 1970s. The main goal was to land a person on the Moon. Success came on July 20, 1969, when astronauts Neil Armstrong and Buzz Aldrin landed a lunar *module named* Eagle *on the Moon.*

Q: What is a lunar module?

A: A lunar module (LM) is a small, light craft that can take off from and land on the Moon. *Eagle* was one of fourteen LMs made for the Apollo project. The success of the project depended on these amazing machines. Some people think that LMs are the greatest engineering achievement of the last hundred years.

Q: How big is a lunar module?

A: Early LMs were about twenty-three feet tall. They measured about thirty feet across and weighed about 32,000 pounds. Later LMs were bigger.

Stop   Think   Write

TEXT AND GRAPHIC FEATURES

How do the photographs on this page help you understand more about the purpose of Project Apollo?

_____

_____

_____

Q: Why did people build lunar modules?

A: Scientists were curious about the Moon. They had many questions about how it was formed. In order to answer the questions, people needed to travel to the Moon. Spacecraft were taking people into space, but they could not land on the Moon. Lunar modules were designed and built to do that job.

Q: Why didn't earlier spaceships land on the Moon?

A: They were too heavy. In the early Apollo trips, astronauts traveled in spacecraft called command modules (CMs). The CMs had to carry astronauts safely back to Earth, but the return trip was perilous. The CMs got very hot as they entered Earth's atmosphere, so they had to have heat shields. The shields made the CMs too heavy to land on the Moon. If people hoped to walk on the Moon, they would need a lighter craft.

A command module

Stop   Think   Write

VOCABULARY

What made the return trip to Earth perilous?

_____

_____

_____

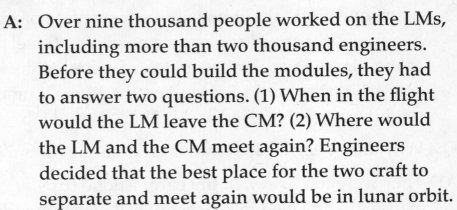

Q: Who designed and made the lunar modules?

A: Over nine thousand people worked on the LMs, including more than two thousand engineers. Before they could build the modules, they had to answer two questions. (1) When in the flight would the LM leave the CM? (2) Where would the LM and the CM meet again? Engineers decided that the best place for the two craft to separate and meet again would be in lunar orbit.

Q: How long did it take to come up with a design?

A: People worked for over five years before the first LM went into space. They started in 1963. Workers researched what the LM would need. Then they designed the parts, built them, and put them together.

Engineers had to make a lot of decisions. Which piece or tool would be lighter? Which would be safer? Which parts were necessary? They had to consider each **option** before making a decision. They performed tests and made changes until they were satisfied.

The first complete LM went into space in 1968. That was a test run. There was no Moon landing. Fourteen lunar modules were built, but only some of them landed on the Moon.

A lunar module on the Moon

Stop Think Write

What did engineers think about as they considered each **option** for the LM?

_____

_____

_____

Q: What happened during a typical Apollo flight?

A: Imagine that you are right there, watching it all. The rocket blasts three astronauts into space. Parts of the rocket fall away until just the command module and the lunar module remain.

After passing behind the Moon, the spacecraft moves into orbit around the Moon. Two astronauts enter the LM, leaving the third astronaut behind in the CM. The lunar module separates from the command module. As it falls toward the Moon, rockets fire. They slow the fall of the LM. The LM seems to be hovering above the surface. At last it lands on the Moon.

The astronauts do tests, gather rocks and dirt, and explore. They also unload anything from the LM that is no longer needed. The craft needs to be as light as possible for the next part of the trip.

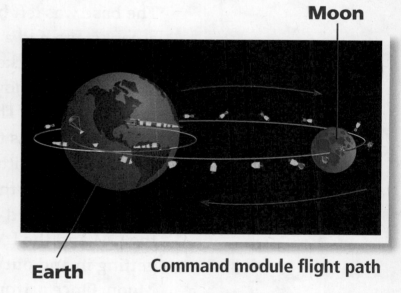

Moon

Earth

Command module flight path

Stop   Think   Write

SEQUENCE OF EVENTS

What happens between the time the spacecraft moves into lunar orbit and the moment the LM lands on the Moon?

_____

_____

_____

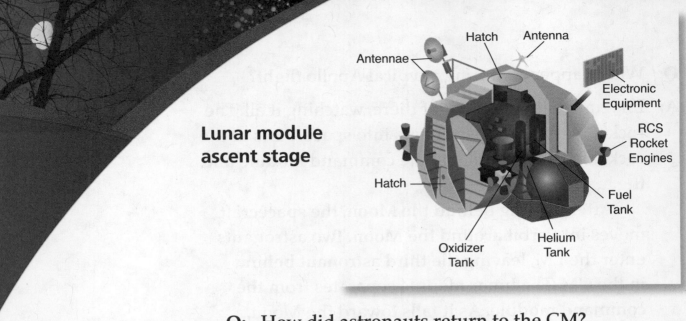

Lunar module ascent stage

Hatch

Antenna

Antennae

Electronic Equipment

RCS Rocket Engines

Hatch

Fuel Tank

Helium Tank

Oxidizer Tank

Q: How did astronauts return to the CM?

A: The top of the lunar module was called the ascent stage. It took astronauts back to the CM. The base was left behind. The outside of the ascent stage had a Rocket Control System (RCS): sixteen small rocket engines that were used for steering. They allowed the pilot to move the LM in any direction. The LM also had antennae. They let the astronauts talk with each other, with the CM, and even with people back on Earth.

Key parts of the LM were its two hatches. The top hatch allowed astronauts to move between the CM and the LM. The side hatch was for getting in and out of the LM when it was on the Moon. Once astronauts returned to the CM, the ascent stage fell back to the Moon.

Stop Think Write

MAIN IDEAS AND DETAILS

What were some key parts of the ascent stage? What was the purpose of each part?

_____

_____

_____

Q: Was the cabin of the LM cramped? Where did the astronauts sit?

A: They didn't. There was no room for seats. The floor space was less than five feet (1.5 m) by five feet (1.5 m), so the astronauts stood up during flights. The LM had oxygen, air pressure, and a comfortable temperature, so the astronauts didn't have to wear their bulky space suits.

Q: Were there any major problems with the LMs?

A: No. The LMs worked very well. They served the Apollo project and took care of the astronauts. This shows the care with which they were designed, built, and tested. It may seem like a shame that most of the LMs had to be left in space.

Q: Where are the Apollo lunar modules today?

A: The table on the next page shows what happened to all fourteen LMs. You can visit the ones that are in museums.

Ascent stage

Lunar module stages

Stop Think Write

TEXT AND GRAPHIC FEATURES

How does the illustration help you understand more about the LM?

_____

_____

_____

Where Are They Now?

LM	Mission	Current Location
1	Apollo 5	Unknown
2	not used	The National Air and Space Museum, Washington, D.C.
3 *Spider*	Apollo 9	Jettisoned in space
4 *Snoopy*	Apollo 10	In orbit around the Sun
5 *Eagle*	Apollo 11	Moon
6 *Intrepid*	Apollo 12	Moon
7 *Aquarius*	Apollo 13	Burned up in Earth's atmosphere
8 *Antares*	Apollo 14	Moon
9	not used	Kennedy Space Center, Orsino, Florida
10 *Falcon*	Apollo 15	Moon
11 *Orion*	Apollo 16	Moon
12 *Challenger*	Apollo 17	Moon
13	not used	The Cradle of Aviation Museum, Garden City, New York
14	not used	The Franklin Institute, Philadelphia, Pennsylvania

Stop Think Write

TEXT AND GRAPHIC FEATURES

Where did many of the lunar modules end up?

150

Look Back and Respond

1 How does the title help you understand the article?

_____

_____

_____

Hint

For clues, see pages 144, 145, and 146.

2 What might scientists hope to learn by sending astronauts to the Moon to do tests, collect samples, and explore?

_____

_____

_____

Hint

For clues, see page 145.

3 Why was the LM's ascent stage so important to the mission?

_____

_____

_____

Hint

For clues, see page 148.

4 How do you think the author feels about lunar modules? Explain.

_____

_____

_____

Hint

For clues, see pages 144 and 149.

Be a Reading Detective!

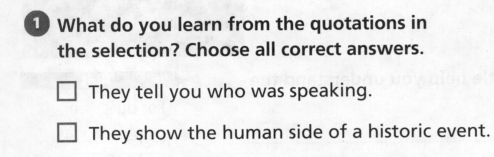

Return to

TEAM MOON
How 400,000 People Landed Apollo 11 on the Moon
CATHERINE THIMMESH

"Team Moon"
Student Book pp. 435–445

1 **What do you learn from the quotations in the selection? Choose all correct answers.**

☐ They tell you who was speaking.

☐ They show the human side of a historic event.

☐ They capture the excitement of the event.

Prove It! What evidence in the selection supports your answer?
Check the boxes. ☑ Make notes.

Evidence	Notes
☐ the quotes about emergencies	
☐ the quotes about the achievement	
☐ quotes about how people felt	

Write About It!

TEXT AND GRAPHIC FEATURES

Answer question **1** using evidence from the text.

_____

_____

_____

_____

_____

_____

_____

2 **The moon landing of the *Eagle* was nearly called off. What was the reason for that?**

☐ The landing gear didn't open.

☐ It was running out of fuel.

☐ The pilot lost control of the module.

Prove It! What evidence in the selection supports your answer? Check the boxes. ☑ Make notes.

Evidence	Notes
☐ the section head "Almost Empty"	
☐ what Mission Control staff said	
☐ statements of how much time was left	

Write About It!

CAUSE AND EFFECT

Answer question 2 using evidence from the text.

_____

_____

_____

_____

_____

_____

ancestral
destiny
ruthless
saga
unearthed

The Vikings

1 The homeland of the Vikings was Scandinavia. Today, Scandinavia includes the countries of Norway, Sweden, and Denmark. In the ninth century, many Vikings left their ancestral lands to settle in Iceland.

Why might people leave their <u>ancestral</u> homes?

_____

_____

_____

2 Vikings carried out raids in foreign lands. They could be ruthless, showing no pity for the people they raided. However, some Vikings were farmers who cared for their families and were merciful to others.

What word in the paragraph is an antonym for <u>ruthless</u>?

_____

3 Erik the Red was a bold Viking who explored and settled in Greenland. The long saga of his life, brave deeds, and adventures has been retold many times.

How is a saga different from other stories?

_____

_____

_____

4 The Vikings tried several times to settle in North America. They may have thought it was their destiny to live there. However, they did not establish a permanent colony. The Vikings eventually left North America.

When we say something is our destiny, what do we mean?

_____

_____

_____

5 Scientists have unearthed the remains of a Viking settlement in North America. Nails, lamps, and other artifacts at the site give clues to how the Vikings lived.

What kinds of things might be unearthed at the site of an ancient settlement?

_____

_____

_____

Erik the Red
and Viking Exploration

by Claire Daniel

Five hundred years before Christopher Columbus "discovered" North America, the Vikings landed there. North America was thousands of miles from the Viking homeland of Scandinavia. However, Viking explorers had a long tradition of traveling beyond their ancestral land. In the eighth and ninth centuries, they led raids to England, Ireland, Wales, and Spain. Viking explorers then sailed from Europe to explore the territory across the Atlantic Ocean.

One of the best-known Viking explorers was Erik the Red. His real name was Eirikr Thorvaldson, but he earned the nickname Erik the Red because of his red hair and beard. His saga has been told for hundreds of years.

Erik was born in Norway around the year 935. When he was still young, his father left Norway with his family. They sailed to Iceland, which had recently been settled by the Vikings. Erik's family built a farm there.

Stop Think Write

What does it mean to call a place your <u>ancestral</u> land?

_____

_____

_____

Westward to Greenland

Erik married a woman from a well-to-do family. As a wedding gift, her father gave the couple a good piece of farmland. Erik's wife said that he was a good husband who farmed well and was kind to her. However, Erik had conflicts with some neighbors that led to violence. In about the year 981, he was banished from Iceland as punishment for his **ruthless** behavior.

Erik the Red set off on a ship, sailing west. He discovered a land that he called Greenland. For a few years, he traveled to different parts of the land. In his opinion, Greenland had even better farmland than Iceland. Erik decided that he wanted to create a permanent settlement in the new land.

Greenland   Iceland

Stop   Think   Write

COMPARE AND CONTRAST

How did Erik's behavior toward his wife differ from his behavior toward his neighbors?

_____

_____

_____

A New Settlement

Erik the Red returned to Iceland, hoping to convince others to join him in Greenland. His stories about the new land excited people. Before long, other Viking families wanted to settle in Greenland.

In 985, Erik led a group of Vikings to Greenland. Men, women, and children boarded twenty-five ships. They brought cattle, sheep, horses, pigs, and dogs with them. They loaded up dried fish and meat, cheese, and butter. They packed farming tools, tents, hunting gear, and kitchen tools.

No one knows how many people left with Erik the Red. Historians think as many as 600 Vikings may have gone. However, the voyage was difficult. Of the twenty-five ships that set off, only fourteen arrived in Greenland. The others either turned back or sank.

Stop Think Write

CONCLUSIONS AND GENERALIZATIONS

Why did the Vikings bring so many animals and supplies with them to Greenland?

_____

_____

_____

An Accidental Discovery

In 986, a trader named Bjarni Herjólfsson left Iceland to join his family in Greenland. He had no compass. His sailors depended on the stars to find their way. Cloudy days and nights made navigation difficult. The sailors veered off course and sailed southwest of Greenland.

There, the trader sighted a new land. Although he did not set foot on the land, he told others about it when he reached Greenland. Many people today believe this new land was what we now call Newfoundland, on the eastern coast of Canada. If so, Herjólfsson had seen North America.

Two people were very interested in the trader's stories: Erik the Red and his son, Leif. Leif offered to buy the trader's ship, and Herjólfsson eventually agreed. Leif wanted to use the ship to sail to the new land that Herjólfsson had seen.

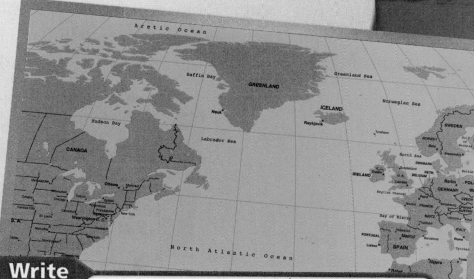

Stop Think Write

INFER AND PREDICT

Explain how Herjólfsson's discovery of the new land was accidental.

_____

_____

_____

Exploring Vinland

Erik the Red intended to travel with his son on this new adventure. However, shortly before the trip was to begin, Erik injured his leg. Viking sailors were very superstitious. Erik thought the broken leg was a bad sign. He may have decided it was not his **destiny** to explore the new land. In the end, he chose not to go on the trip.

Leif reached the new land and sailed south along the coast. First, he saw a land that had flat stones, which was probably the Baffin Islands. He kept sailing. Next, he saw a wooded land with a white beach. He called it "Markland." It was probably the south shore of Labrador.

Leif sailed on until he reached a third place. This land had fields, woods, pastures, and grapevines. He called it "Vinland." Leif and his crew stepped ashore at Vinland. They became the first Europeans to set foot on American soil. They spent the winter at Vinland before returning to Greenland.

Stop Think Write

Why might Erik the Red have thought it was not his <u>destiny</u> to explore the new land?

_____

_____

_____

A Family of Explorers

Erik the Red had four children: Leif, Thorvald, Thorstein, and Freydis. They all left Greenland to explore North America. After Leif's return, Thorvald sailed to Vinland and explored the nearby coasts. He fought with local American Indians. During one fight, an arrow struck and killed him.

Leif's brother Thorstein led another group of Vikings to America, but they did not stay. Yet another group of Vikings tried to establish a colony in Vinland, but fighting with American Indians proved too dangerous. The group packed up and left.

Erik the Red's daughter, Freydis, was part of a later group that tried to settle in Vinland. Fighting led to the failure of this settlement, too. However, the fighting wasn't against American Indians. People from Iceland fought against people from Greenland!

Despite many tries, the Vikings couldn't create a permanent colony in Vinland. Even so, the adventures of Erik the Red and his family have been told over and over since that time.

Stop   Think   Write

COMPARE AND CONTRAST

How were the troubles of Freydis's group different from problems encountered by previous Viking groups in Vinland?

_____

_____

_____

Where Was Vinland?

No one knows the exact location of Vinland. Some people think it was where Cape Cod, Massachusetts, is now. Others believe it was in Newfoundland, Canada.

*****

In 1960, scientists unearthed remains of a Viking colony in Newfoundland. The scientists found eight buildings at the site. They also found boat sheds and large outdoor pits for cooking meat. Among the artifacts at the site were nails, a lamp, an anvil stone, and a spindle. The spindle proved that women lived there and used the spindle to spin wool into yarn.

Today you can visit the remains of the Viking settlement. It is called L'Anse aux Meadows. Many people think the settlement must be Vinland, but there is no way to know for sure.

Stop Think Write

MAIN IDEAS AND DETAILS

Which artifact helps us understand the role that women played in the Viking settlement we now call L'Anse aux Meadows? Explain.

_____

_____

_____

Look Back and Respond

1 **Who was Paris?**

_____

_____

_____

Hint

For a clue, see page 175.

2 **Why did King Agamemnon sail to Troy with Greek troops?**

_____

_____

_____

Hint

For a clue, see page 175.

3 **How did the Trojans get the massive horse through the gate?**

_____

_____

_____

Hint

For a clue, see page 179.

4 **How might archaeologists finally prove that the Trojan horse was real?**

_____

_____

_____

Hint

Think about evidence you would need to convince you.

Be a Reading Detective!

Return to

ROBERT BYRD

the HERO and the MINOTAUR

"The Hero
and the Minotaur"
Student Book pp. 523–535

1 **Think about the problems Theseus faces.**
Is every problem solved?

☐ yes

☐ no

Prove It! What evidence in the story supports your answer?
Check the boxes. Make notes.

Evidence	Notes
☐ Theseus' problem with the Minotaur	
☐ what Theseus does to the Minotaur	
☐ what Theseus forgets to do at the end	
☐	

Write About It!

STORY STRUCTURE

Answer question 1 using evidence from the text.

_____

_____

_____

_____

_____

_____

2 **Which theme best describes what happens in "The Hero and the Minotaur"?**

☐ Children can be cruel to their parents.

☐ Bravery and goodness are rewarded.

☐ Heroes never need help from others to succeed.

☐ other _____

Prove It! What evidence in the story supports your answer? Check the boxes. ☑ Make notes.

Evidence	Notes
☐ Theseus' actions	
☐ other characters' actions	
☐	

Write About It!

THEME

Answer question 2 using evidence from the text.

_____

_____

_____

_____

_____

_____

_____

TARGET VOCABULARY

**ceremonial
divine
erected
fragments
pondered**

Ancient Cultures

Check the answer.

1 Every culture has its _____ objects. These are items that are used at events such as births, weddings, deaths, and the appointment of new rulers. Each object has a special purpose and meaning.

☐ **pondered** ☐ **erected** ☐ **ceremonial**

2 In some ancient cultures, people believed that their rulers were _____. The ruler was thought to be more like a god than like an ordinary person.

☐ **divine** ☐ **ceremonial** ☐ **lustrous**

3 In every age, people have _____ monuments and statues. We build these things to honor a person or to remember an important event in history. For example, the Great Pyramids of Egypt were raised as tombs for ancient Egyptian kings.

☐ **affirmed** ☐ **erected** ☐ **divine**

4 Lucy could not remember doing anything spiteful to Mara. Lucy had not said anything on purpose to hurt Mara or make her angry.

Was Lucy's comment about Beth meant to be spiteful toward Mara? Explain.

_____

_____

_____

5 Eventually, Lucy asked Mara why she was angry. When Lucy realized what she had done, she felt terrible.

If you are not nice to a friend, what might eventually happen to the friendship?

_____

_____

_____

Everyone's Favorite Music

by Mia Lewis

Jay Kovak and Julio Santiago lived in a neighborhood with people of all different cultures and national backgrounds. People spoke English, but you could also hear Chinese, Portuguese, Russian, Creole, Laotian, and more than one kind of Spanish.

Every summer, the neighbors had a big party. There was always lots of food, fun, and music! Neighbors took turns hosting the party. This summer, it was the Santiago family's turn.

Julio was excited. His mom put him in charge of the music. Last year, the Kovaks hosted the party. Jay had planned the music—with Julio's help, of course.

Jay and Julio had been best friends since they were in preschool. Now they were in the same sixth-grade class, and still best friends. Julio had a new friend named Eli Jones. Julio was planning to ask Eli to help with the music, too.

Stop Think Write

COMPARE AND CONTRAST

How is the preparation for this year's party different from last year's?

_____

_____

_____

Mrs. Santiago was concerned about the boys' choice of music. "The music is supposed to *entertain* people," she reminded them. "It should make them sing and dance. The music is for *everyone*."

"Don't worry, Mami," said Julio. "This party is going to be the best ever! The three of us will have fun working together. Right, Jay? Right, Eli?"

"Right!" said Eli. "I know all the hottest hits. Leave it to me, Mrs. Santiago."

Jay said nothing. He didn't think it would be fun working with Eli. Eli didn't even live in the neighborhood.

Mrs. Santiago could sense Jay's concern. She worried that three boys might be one too many for this project. She hoped Julio's friendship with Jay wasn't in jeopardy.

Stop   Think   Write

COMPARE AND CONTRAST

How does Julio feel about the three boys working together? How does Jay feel?

_____

_____

_____

205

"Let's have lots of Latin music, because it's best for dancing," announced Julio, as the three began planning.

"Latin music is great," agreed Jay. "The neighbors loved that music from last year's party. And let's include some R & B favorites for our parents."

"Are you guys kidding?" asked Eli. "We don't want that old stuff! We've got to play what's hot—the hip-hop songs from the top of the charts."

"Who asked you?" **blurted** out Jay. "Our neighbors don't like that kind of music!"

Jay was not a **spiteful** person, but he didn't like Eli's I-know-best attitude. It bothered him that Julio was letting Eli have a say in their party. He wished that just Julio and he were planning the music, like last year.

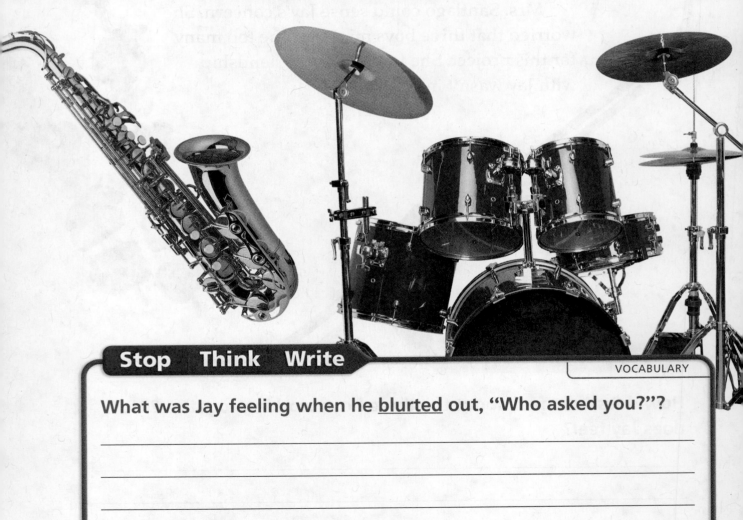

Stop   Think   Write

What was Jay feeling when he **blurted** out, "Who asked you?"?

_____

_____

_____

"Hold on," said Julio calmly. "There's no need to get mad. Lots of people enjoy hip-hop, Jay. That's why it's at the top of the charts, buddy! Even *I* like it!"

"That's right!" said Eli, sounding proud of himself, as if he were the winner of a competition. "Everything changes, you know."

"But, Eli, I like Latin music, too. And my mom likes R & B," said Julio. "Lots of different people are coming to this party, so we should have music for everyone— disco, funk, mambo, country, R & B, *and* rap. Our neighborhood is all about diversity."

"Yeah," said Jay, nodding in agreement at Julio's idea. "Our neighborhood is a mix of all types! We have to play a mix of music that *all* of our neighbors will enjoy."

Stop Think Write

COMPARE AND CONTRAST

Compare and contrast Eli's ideas about music for the party with Julio's and Jay's ideas.

_____

_____

_____

207

Eli was quiet for a while, and he seemed to be thinking hard. **Eventually**, he spoke.

"You guys are right," said Eli. "The music is not about what's hot. It's about what people like. Don't forget what Julio's mom said. The music should get *everyone* dancing and singing. How do we know what kind of dance music everyone likes, though? Maybe there's Chinese dance music we don't know about. Or Brazilian. Also, what about that grumpy guy who lives on the corner? What kind of music do you think *he* likes?"

Jay smiled. Eli was talking about Mr. Bromley. He always sat on his front porch, frowning at everyone who passed by. He greeted kids by barking an **abrupt** warning: "You kids stay off my grass!" If Eli had noticed Mr. Bromley, maybe he was getting to know the neighborhood better than Jay had thought!

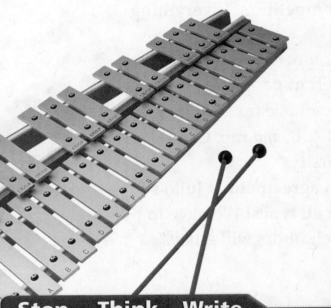

Stop Think Write

VOCABULARY

In the last paragraph, why is Mr. Bromley's greeting described as <u>abrupt</u>?

_____

_____

_____

"It's kind of you to think of Mr. Bromley," said Julio, "but let's face it. There's no way we can include the favorite music of every single person in the neighborhood."

"True," said Jay, "but I agree that it's a nice idea."

"It's more than an idea," said Eli with a smile. "If we work together, we can make it happen!"

Eli had a plan. The boys would ask each neighbor for a recording of his or her favorite music. Then they would make a compilation! The final CD would really be *everyone's* favorite music!

Jay had to admit that Eli's idea was brilliant. Eli had been willing to change his mind about what music to play. Maybe it was time for Jay to change his mind about Eli.

Stop Think Write

INFER AND PREDICT.

Why does Jay think Eli's idea is brilliant?

_____

_____

_____

The boys carried out Eli's plan. They went from house to house, gathering music. By the time they finished, they had collected fifty-year-old records, twenty-five-year-old tapes, CDs, and digital files on flash drives. The music was a true mix of generations and cultures.

Jay enjoyed listening to the different music. He even liked working with Eli. He was beginning to see why Julio was friends with him.

That year, the neighborhood party was hot in every way. The July sun was hot. The food was hot and spicy, thanks to Mami's Latin cooking. Most of all, the dance music was hot, hot, hot!

Everyone danced, even Mr. Bromley.

Stop Think Write

COMPARE AND CONTRAST

How does the music at this year's party differ from the music in previous years?

_____

_____

_____

Look Back and Respond

1 Mrs. Santiago is worried about two things at the beginning of the story. What are they?

_____

_____

_____

Hint

For clues, look on page 205.

2 At first, what kind of music do Julio and Jay think they should play at the party? How does this compare to what Eli thinks?

_____

_____

_____

Hint

For clues, see page 206.

3 How does Eli's idea for party music change? Why does it change?

_____

_____

_____

Hint

For clues, see pages 207 and 208.

4 Compare and contrast how Jay feels about Eli at the beginning and at the end of the story.

_____

_____

_____

Hint

For clues, see pages 205, 206, 209, and 210.

Be a Reading Detective!

Return to

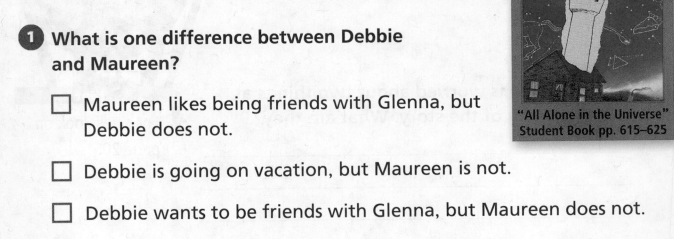

"All Alone in the Universe"
Student Book pp. 615–625

1 **What is one difference between Debbie and Maureen?**

☐ Maureen likes being friends with Glenna, but Debbie does not.

☐ Debbie is going on vacation, but Maureen is not.

☐ Debbie wants to be friends with Glenna, but Maureen does not.

Prove It! What evidence in the story supports your answer?
Check the boxes. ☑ Make notes.

Evidence	Notes
☐ Maureen's words and actions	
☐ Debbie's thoughts	
☐ Debbie's words and actions	

Write About It!

COMPARE AND CONTRAST

Answer question 1 using evidence from the text.

_____

_____

_____

_____

_____

_____

2 **On page 621, what does Debbie mean when she says that "the water rose over my little island"?**

☐ She feels even more separated from Maureen.

☐ She feels as if she lives on an island.

☐ other _____

Prove It! What evidence in the story supports your answer? Check the boxes. ☑ Make notes.

Evidence	Notes
☐ Debbie's thoughts a few moments earlier	
☐ the events of the day	
☐	

Write About It!

FIGURATIVE LANGUAGE

Answer question 2 using evidence from the text.

_____

_____

_____

_____

_____

_____

_____

211B

Early Attempts to Fly

✓ **TARGET VOCABULARY**

conditions
decrepit
frustration
harsh
instinct

1 A bird knows how to fly by **instinct**. It is born knowing how to flap its wings. Flying comes naturally for a bird.

Describe something else an animal might do by <u>instinct</u>.

_____

_____

_____

2 Throughout history, people have dreamed of flying. Early efforts were met with **frustration**. The first flying machines did not work very well.

What causes you <u>frustration</u>?

_____

_____

_____

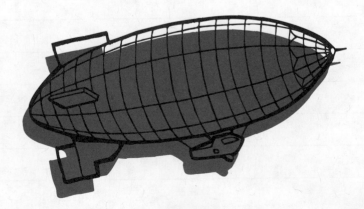

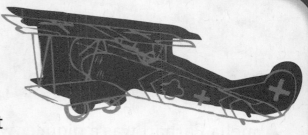

3 Some early inventors made aircraft from very light materials that would float on the air currents. These aircraft often fell apart in strong, harsh winds.

Write an antonym for harsh.

_____

4 Inventors looked for places with perfect conditions to test their aircraft. The wind speed and direction had to be just right to lift the aircraft off the ground.

What are the best conditions for doing homework?

_____

_____

_____

5 Aircraft can become worn and decrepit over time. They might fall apart completely if they aren't carefully maintained.

What else can become decrepit over time? Why?

_____

Amelia Earhart
Pioneer Pilot

by K.C. Archer

Amelia Earhart was a pioneer who changed how people thought about flying and pilots. She changed how people thought about what women can do.

Amelia Earhart was born on July 24, 1897. She saw her first plane at a state fair when she was ten years old. She was not impressed by the rusty and decrepit aircraft.

When she was twenty, Amelia went to a stunt-flying show with a friend. The pilots performed tricks in their airplanes. A pilot saw Amelia and her friend, and he tried to scare the women by flying straight at them. Amelia did not move an inch.

Instead of being afraid, Amelia was fascinated. She knew then that flying was her future.

Stop Think Write

VOCABULARY

What might a decrepit aircraft look like?

_____

_____

_____

214

Young Amelia

Friends were not surprised by Amelia's interest in planes. Amelia was always looking for adventure, and she liked to do things that were off-limits for women at that time. She kept a scrapbook of articles about pioneering women. Most of the articles were about women in engineering, law, and other male-dominated fields. Amelia knew that women were just as smart and capable as men were. She wanted to prove this to the world.

Amelia graduated from high school in 1915. She worked as a nurse's aid in Canada during World War I, taking care of wounded soldiers. Later, she went to college and then got a job as a social worker. She began to save money.

Stop   Think   Write

CONCLUSIONS AND GENERALIZATIONS

What details help you conclude that Amelia Earhart was different from most women of her time?

_____

_____

_____

Flying the *Canary*

January 3, 1921, was a day that changed Amelia's life forever. On that day, she had her first flying lesson. Amelia loved to fly and learned quickly. She had an **instinct** for flying.

Six months after she began flying, Amelia bought her own plane. It was small and yellow and fit only two people. She called it *Canary*.

In October of 1922, Amelia flew 14,000 feet high in her plane. It was the first time a woman had flown that high! Already Amelia was breaking records, but rather than joy, she felt **frustration**. She had set a world record, but no one paid attention. Although the world didn't think of her as a great pilot, Amelia didn't give up. She kept her job as a social worker and flew her plane as a hobby. Her big break came a few years later.

Stop   Think   Write

CONCLUSIONS AND GENERALIZATIONS

Why didn't the world think of Amelia Earhart as a great pilot?

_____

_____

_____

A Dream Come True

In 1928, Amelia got a phone call from a man who asked if she would like to fly across the Atlantic Ocean. Amelia was thrilled, but she wondered if the call was a trick. Why would anyone ask *her* to fly on such a dangerous and important mission?

Amelia learned that the call was real and said yes. She went to New York and met the people who would fly across the Atlantic with her. Her copilot, Wilmer "Bill" Stultz, was well known and respected. Louis E. "Slim" Gordon would be on board as the mechanic. His job was to fix anything that went wrong with the plane during the flight.

Stop Think Write

CONCLUSIONS AND GENERALIZATIONS

Why might Amelia Earhart have thought the phone call was not real?

_____

_____

_____

A World-Famous Journey

On June 17, 1928, Amelia, Bill, and Slim took off from the east coast of Canada. They flew a small plane called *Friendship*. The plane was faster than other airplanes of the time. Even so, it took almost twenty-one hours to reach Great Britain. The journey was long and difficult, and conditions on the little plane were harsh. Amelia and her crew flew through fog and lightning and were blown off course by strong winds.

When they arrived in Great Britain, Amelia, Bill, and Slim were instantly famous. People around the world heard the story of their journey. At last, Amelia received recognition for her daring and skill.

Amelia was happy, but she wanted to do more. She decided to spend her time setting new world records. From then on, the sky was the limit.

Stop   Think   Write

VOCABULARY

What was harsh about the flight across the Atlantic?

_____

_____

_____

Breaking Records

In 1929, Amelia joined the National Aeronautic Association. She wanted to create separate flying records for women. She set and broke many of those records herself, including the record for fastest speed in an airplane.

In 1932, Amelia made a second journey across the Atlantic. This time she traveled alone. She was the first woman to fly solo across the Atlantic Ocean. The trip took just fourteen hours and fifty-six minutes.

Later that year, Amelia set a record for speed. She flew across the United States in nineteen hours and five minutes. In 1933, she repeated the flight, breaking her own record for time. Two years later, Amelia flew more than 2,400 miles from California to Hawaii. There was no stopping her.

People's shock at her daring feats made Amelia push even harder. She was always ready for new and exciting challenges.

Stop Think Write

CAUSE AND EFFECT

What caused Amelia Earhart to try even harder to break records?

_____

_____

_____

What Happened to Amelia Earhart?

When Amelia Earhart was nearly forty years old, she decided to fly around the world. This journey would be her most dangerous yet.

Her flight began in Florida. For a month, Amelia flew east. She stopped in Africa, in India, and finally in Papua, New Guinea.

The last part of the journey was across the Pacific Ocean. During the flight, Amelia lost touch with the U.S. Coast Guard. Her plane disappeared. A rescue mission searched for Amelia day after day. They found nothing.

To this day, no one knows for sure what happened.

Amelia Earhart is remembered as a woman who changed the world. She was a true pioneer of aviation.

Stop Think Write

UNDERSTANDING CHARACTERS

What made Amelia Earhart a pioneer?

_____

_____

_____

Look Back and Respond

1 Flying was a dangerous occupation when Amelia Earhart was young. Why weren't friends surprised that she was interested in flying?

_____

_____

_____

> **Hint**
> For clues, see page 215.

2 Why did Amelia Earhart like the challenge of setting and breaking records?

_____

_____

_____

> **Hint**
> For clues, see pages 214, 215, 216, 218, and 219.

3 Overall, how did Amelia Earhart live her life?

_____

_____

_____

> **Hint**
> Clues are on almost every page!

4 In what ways do you think Amelia Earhart changed what people thought women could achieve?

_____

_____

_____

> **Hint**
> Think about all the things Amelia Earhart did.

Be a Reading Detective!

Return to

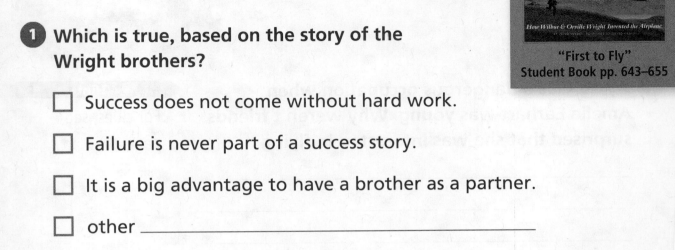

FIRST to FLY

How Wilbur & Orville Wright Invented the Airplane

"First to Fly"
Student Book pp. 643–655

1 **Which is true, based on the story of the Wright brothers?**

☐ Success does not come without hard work.

☐ Failure is never part of a success story.

☐ It is a big advantage to have a brother as a partner.

☐ other _____

Prove It! What evidence in the selection supports your answer?
Check the boxes. ☑ Make notes.

Evidence	Notes
☐ events at Kitty Hawk	
☐ events at home	
☐ failed attempts to fly	

Write About It!

CONCLUSIONS AND GENERALIZATIONS

Answer question 1 using evidence from the text.

_____

_____

_____

_____

_____

_____

_____

2 **What does the heading "Twelve Magic Seconds" describe?**

☐ the longest flight the Wrights made

☐ how long the first powered flight lasted

☐ other _____

Prove It! What evidence in the selection supports your answer? Check the boxes. ☑ Make notes.

Evidence	Notes
☐ Wilbur's use of his stopwatch	
☐ details about the airplane	
☐ the events of December 17	

Write About It!

MAIN IDEAS AND DETAILS

Answer question 2 using evidence from the text.

_____

_____

_____

_____

_____

_____

contempt
exasperated
intently
scornfully
subsided

A TIME OF WAR

On December 7, 1941, Japanese planes attacked Pearl Harbor, Hawaii. America declared war on Japan, and then Germany declared war on the United States. America had entered World War II. American soldiers fought **intently** against the enemy.

Many Japanese Americans and German Americans lived in the United States. Some other Americans were suspicious and felt hatred and **contempt**. They acted **scornfully** toward Japanese Americans and German Americans. Some people feared that Japanese Americans might help Japan, so the government made Japanese Americans live in internment camps.

Many Japanese Americans became **exasperated** with the cramped conditions and suspicion they had to endure. However, they had to stay in the camps until Japan surrendered in 1945. Once fears **subsided**, the camps were closed.

1 Some fearful Americans acted

_____

towards Americans from Japan and Germany.

2 Japanese Americans became

_____ with conditions in

internment camps.

3 Camps for Japanese Americans closed when fears

_____.

4 When you are determined to do something, you act <u>intently</u>. Describe the last time you acted intently. What were you doing?

_____

_____

_____

5 Why might a person feel <u>contempt</u> for another person?

_____

_____

_____

IT'S MY COUNTRY, TOO

By Margaret Maugenest

Life was good for my family in 1941. We owned a small hotel in Los Angeles. My brother, Joe, was ten. I was twelve. We were typical American children who did well in school and played with our friends. Joe liked baseball, and I took art classes.

My parents, Kenji and Izumi Natsumi, were born in Japan. They got married in their twenties, and then they moved to the United States. They worked at a factory and saved every penny. With the help of a bank loan, they bought the hotel.

We lived in a small house. My father worked hard at the hotel, and my mom took care of our home. Joe and I loved to be at the hotel, and we enjoyed meeting the many people who stayed there.

Stop Think Write

CAUSE AND EFFECT

What were the narrator's parents able to do because they had worked hard and saved?

_____

_____

_____

On December 7, 1941, our lives changed forever.

Joe and I were playing catch when our mother yelled to us, "Sue, Joe, come inside!" As we entered the house, we could hear the news on the radio. There had been an attack at Pearl Harbor, Hawaii. We knew the U.S. Navy had many ships there. "The United States has been attacked by the Japanese," said my mother. Joe and I looked at each other, not sure what to think.

The phone rang. It was my father. I overheard my mother talking and crying. We stayed in the house all day, listening to the radio and worrying.

The next day, Joe and I walked to school as usual. We ran into Joe's friend Sam. Sam looked down. "My mom says I can't play with you anymore."

Stop Think Write

CAUSE AND EFFECT

Why did the narrator's mother tell Sue and Joe to come inside?

_____

_____

_____

Joe didn't understand why Sam said this. I thought, "It must be because of the Japanese bombing the ships. How can Sam's mom think we had anything to do with that? We're Americans. We were born here."

Before long, the United States entered World War II, fighting against Germany and Japan. Everyone was nervous and upset about the war. Some people looked at us with contempt, even though they had no reason to hate us. They treated us scornfully, as if we had done something horrible. It made me very sad.

In March 1942, my mother gave us some horrible news. The U.S. government was forcing Japanese Americans in some western states out of their homes. Some people worried that Japan was going to attack the West Coast and that Japanese people living there would help.

Stop Think Write

Why did some people start treating the narrator's family with contempt after December 7, 1941?

_____

_____

_____

"Where are we supposed to go?" I asked.

"I don't know," my mother replied.

"How long will we be gone?" Joe wanted to know.

"No one knows," she responded sadly.

My mother and father discussed the situation with friends. They learned that there would be ten internment camps where Japanese Americans would be forced to live. We had only a few weeks to leave our homes and report to a camp.

Over the next three weeks, we sold most of our belongings—our car, furniture, books, and house. Father was forced to sell the hotel for a very low price. Our neighbor, Mrs. Daniels, let us store some things in her basement. Mostly we just kept clothing to wear at the camp. I had never cried so much. My nice life was quickly becoming awful.

Stop Think Write

CAUSE AND EFFECT

Why did the family sell most of their belongings and the hotel?

_____

_____

_____

At the end of the month, we boarded a train to eastern California. We were assigned to a camp called Manzanar.

When we arrived there, guards searched and questioned us intently. We were assigned a tiny barrack to live in. Inside were small, straw mattresses. My father was furious, but he just sat down and said nothing.

A barbed-wire fence surrounded the camp. There were armed guards all around to make sure no one left. Over ten thousand Japanese Americans were living there. All of them were wondering why they were forced to live like this *in their own country*. They had done nothing wrong. Some people felt exasperated with the unfair situation.

I tried to write poems to make myself feel better. Months passed, and we managed, but I felt sad for the very little boys and girls forced to live in the camp.

Stop   Think   Write

How did Sue feel about being in the Manzanar camp?

_____

_____

_____

By the spring of 1944, America was winning the war. Fear that Japanese Americans would help Japan **subsided**. At the start of 1945, the U.S. government announced that it would close the camps by the end of the year. All the people would be free to go.

We were happy, but worried. What would it be like when we returned home? How would other Americans treat us? Where would we live, and what would we do? We had lost our house, our belongings, and the hotel.

In April 1945, we finally left Manzanar. Our old neighbor, Mrs. Daniels, picked us up at the train station in Los Angeles. We were headed to Long Beach, where my uncle lived. He had been in a camp, too, but neighbors had taken care of his house. We were going to stay with him until we were settled in our new lives.

Stop Think Write

VOCABULARY

What happened when the fear of Japanese Americans <u>subsided</u>?

_____

_____

_____

On our way to Long Beach, Joe asked, "Mrs. Daniels, will you drive us by our old house?"

My parents looked at each other. They wanted to see the house, but they also *didn't* want to see it. My father nodded to Mrs. Daniels, and we drove there.

Our street looked the same. We had sold the house to an older couple, and Mrs. Daniels said they had taken good care of it. Still, none of us could keep from feeling sad when we drove past it. I also felt anger, since my parents had worked so hard for that house, and they had lost it just because we were Japanese Americans.

At first, it was hard getting back to our old lives. Eventually life settled back to normal, at least a new normal. We would never forget our experience, but we had survived, and we were still together.

Stop Think Write

CAUSE AND EFFECT

Why did the narrator feel anger when she saw her old house?

_____

_____

_____

Look Back and Respond

1 Why did the U.S. government put Japanese Americans in internment camps?

_____

_____

_____

For clues, see pages 226 and 227.

2 What effect did going to the camps have on the family in the story?

_____

_____

_____

Hint

For clues, see pages 227, 228, and 229.

3 How did seeing their old house make Sue and her family feel?

_____

_____

_____

Hint

For a clue, see page 230.

4 How can you tell that the writer's family had strength and courage?

_____

_____

_____

Hint

Clues you can use are on almost every page.

Be a Reading Detective!

Return to

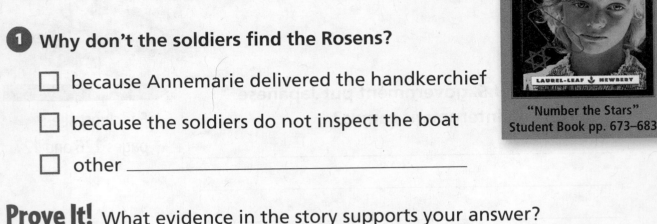

"Number the Stars"
Student Book pp. 673–683

1 **Why don't the soldiers find the Rosens?**

☐ because Annemarie delivered the handkerchief

☐ because the soldiers do not inspect the boat

☐ other _____

Prove It! What evidence in the story supports your answer?
Check the boxes. ☑ Make notes.

Evidence	Notes
☐ details about the Nazis' dogs	
☐ details about what Annemarie delivered	
☐ what Uncle Henrik tells Annemarie	

Write About It!

CAUSE AND EFFECT

Answer question 1 using evidence from the text.

_____

_____

_____

_____

_____

_____

2 **Annemarie doesn't think that she is brave. What do you think?**

☐ Annemarie isn't brave because she is frightened.

☐ Annemarie is brave.

Prove It! What evidence in the story supports your answer? Check the boxes. ☑ Make notes.

Evidence	Notes
☐ how Annemarie speaks to the Nazis	
☐ what Uncle Henrik says about bravery	
☐	

Write About It!

Answer question 2 using evidence from the text.

_____

_____

_____

_____

_____

_____

✓ **TARGET VOCABULARY**

destination
inexplicable
intention
legitimate
motioned

Getting Out the Vote

In 1964, I was twenty years old. When I told my family that my **1** _____ was to register voters, or sign people up to vote, they were happy at first. They knew that some people needed help. Then I told them I was leaving our state to do this. My **2** _____ was Mississippi. Their faces fell. Mom **3** _____ to me to step out of the room. She said that my plans were puzzling and even **4** _____. Why would I would want to travel so far away, even for a good cause? I explained that I thought it was right, or **5** _____, to travel far away to help people. My mother finally agreed with me. She hugged me, and then she helped me pack.

6 Our mayor announced her _____

to run for governor, and reporters spread the news.

7 She rode in a bus all over the state, but her

final _____ was the state capital.

8 At one press conference, she

_____ with her hand

to a reporter.

9 The reporter asked whether she thought the city

had a _____ reason to cut funds

to hospitals.

10 She could not think of a good reason for the move

and said that it was _____ to her.

Sitting In for Rights

by Judy Rosenbaum

Imagine that you and your family went shopping downtown. Maybe you bought school supplies or looked for new shoes. After several hours of shopping, you were hungry and thirsty.

The store you just spent so much money in had a lunch counter. You all sat down to order a snack. But the person behind the counter **motioned** for you to get up and leave. You and your family were not allowed to eat at that lunch counter—ever.

Stop   Think   Write

AUTHOR'S PURPOSE

Why do you think the author begins by asking readers to imagine going shopping?

_____

_____

_____

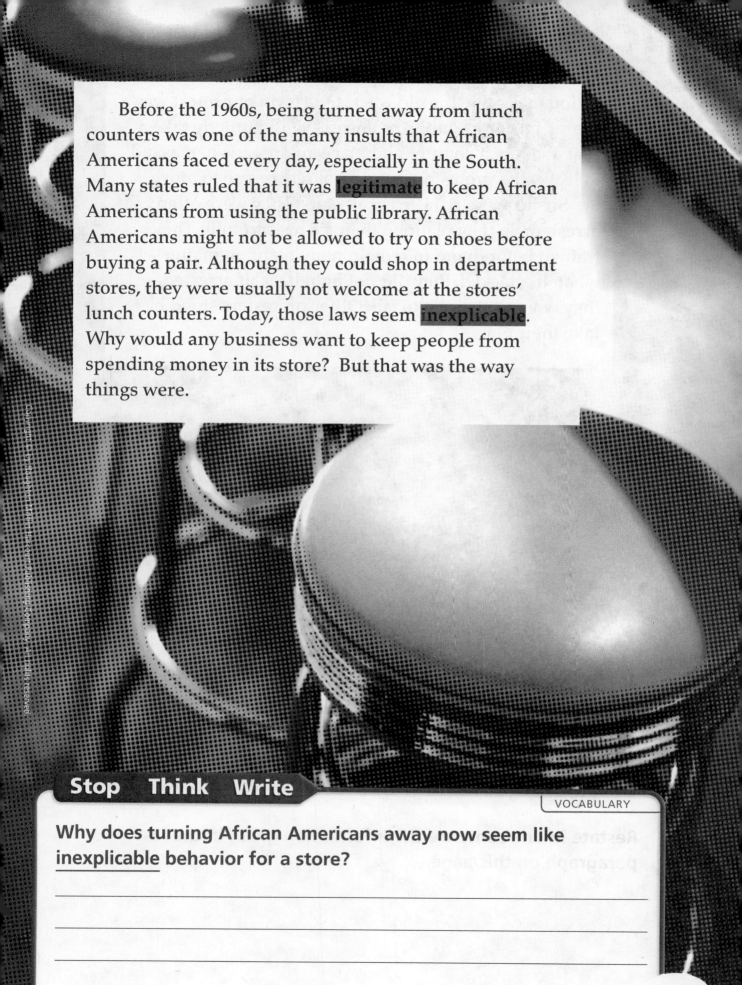

Before the 1960s, being turned away from lunch counters was one of the many insults that African Americans faced every day, especially in the South. Many states ruled that it was **legitimate** to keep African Americans from using the public library. African Americans might not be allowed to try on shoes before buying a pair. Although they could shop in department stores, they were usually not welcome at the stores' lunch counters. Today, those laws seem **inexplicable**. Why would any business want to keep people from spending money in its store? But that was the way things were.

Stop Think Write

VOCABULARY

Why does turning African Americans away now seem like <u>inexplicable</u> behavior for a store?

_____

_____

_____

By the early 1960s, people were taking nonviolent action to change the old ways. One form of protest was the sit-in. For example, protesters would quietly take a seat at a lunch counter and place an order. When asked to leave, the protesters would politely refuse to move.

Sit-ins were risky for protesters. They were often arrested. So they planned their sit-ins carefully. They trained beforehand to remain nonviolent no matter what. If attacked, they did not fight back. If arrested, they went peacefully to jail. Other protesters stood by to take their places.

MAIN IDEAS AND DETAILS

Restate in one sentence the information given in the last paragraph on this page.

_____

_____

_____

The first sit-in of the modern civil-rights movement took place in Greensboro, North Carolina, on February 1, 1960. Four college students showed up on North Elm Street. Their **destination** was the lunch counter at Woolworth's. When they sat down, the waitress refused to serve them. The protesters remained seated until the store closed.

In time, more students protested in Greensboro. The protests spread to other stores. The word spread through the South and then through the country, by newspaper reports and phone calls to other colleges. College students, both black and white, began large-scale sit-ins in Nashville, Tennessee, and many other cities.

Stop Think Write

SEQUENCE OF EVENTS

Summarize what happened in Greensboro, using the words *first*, *next*, *then*, and *after that*.

_____

_____

_____

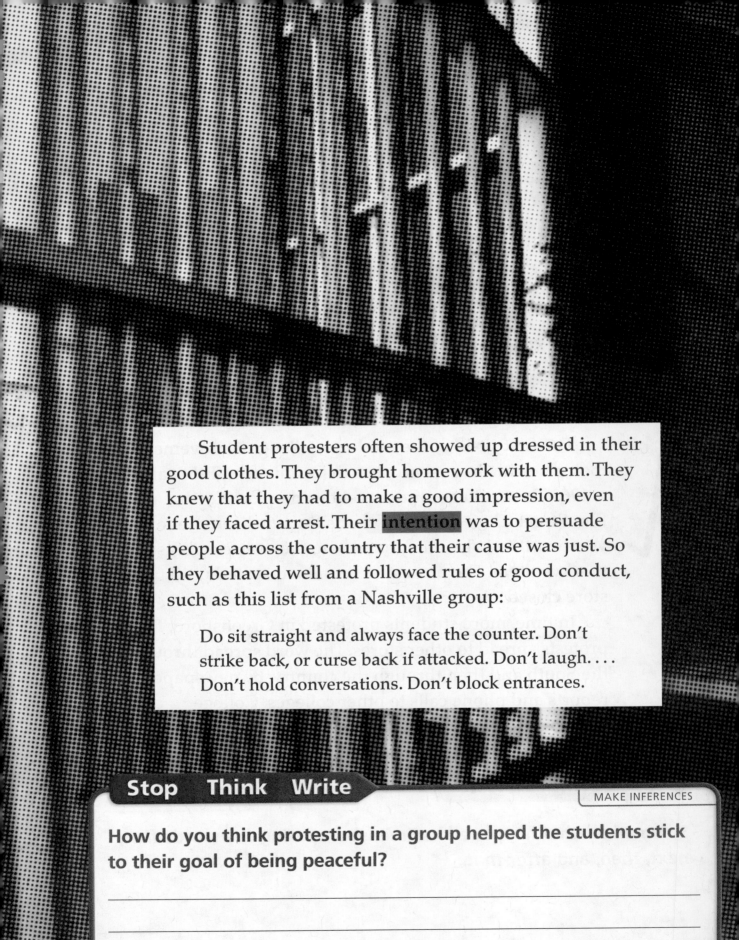

Student protesters often showed up dressed in their good clothes. They brought homework with them. They knew that they had to make a good impression, even if they faced arrest. Their **intention** was to persuade people across the country that their cause was just. So they behaved well and followed rules of good conduct, such as this list from a Nashville group:

> Do sit straight and always face the counter. Don't strike back, or curse back if attacked. Don't laugh. . . . Don't hold conversations. Don't block entrances.

Stop **Think** **Write**

MAKE INFERENCES

How do you think protesting in a group helped the students stick to their goal of being peaceful?

_____

_____

_____

Newpapers all over the country carried stories and photographs about the sit-ins. Americans could see that the students were being peaceful. They could see that the students just wanted people to have equal rights. More and more people started to agree with the students' cause.

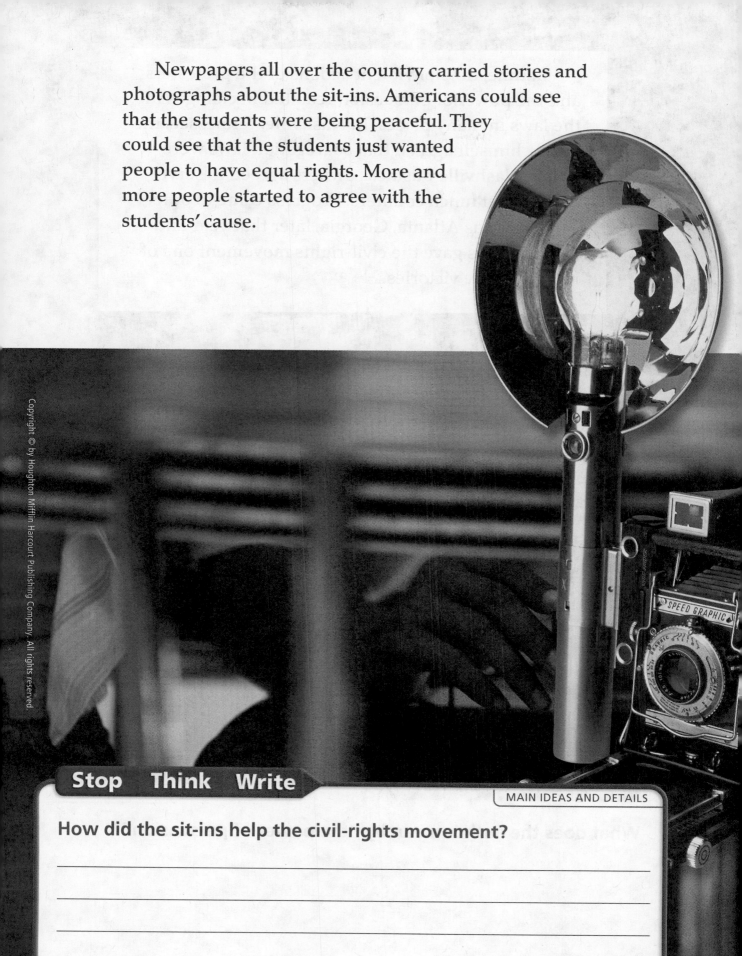

Stop Think Write

MAIN IDEAS AND DETAILS

How did the sit-ins help the civil-rights movement?

_____

_____

_____

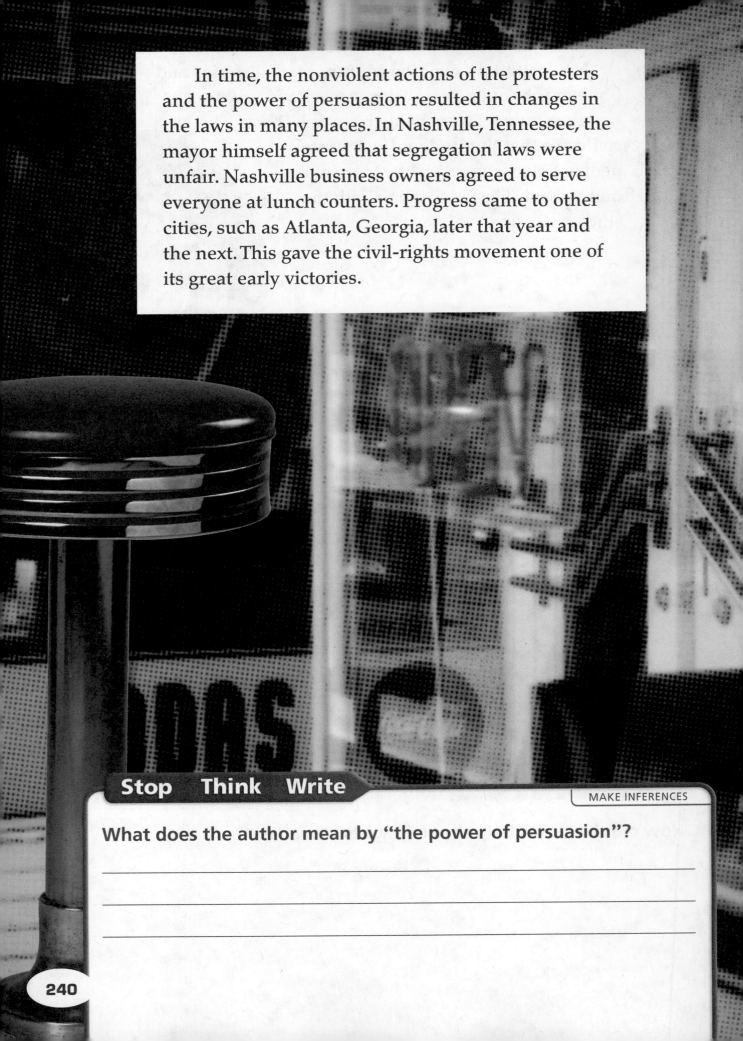

In time, the nonviolent actions of the protesters and the power of persuasion resulted in changes in the laws in many places. In Nashville, Tennessee, the mayor himself agreed that segregation laws were unfair. Nashville business owners agreed to serve everyone at lunch counters. Progress came to other cities, such as Atlanta, Georgia, later that year and the next. This gave the civil-rights movement one of its great early victories.

Stop Think Write

MAKE INFERENCES

What does the author mean by "the power of persuasion"?

_____

_____

_____

1 **What is the purpose of this selection?**

_____

_____

_____

2 **How does the author describe segregation in the 1960s in this selection?**

_____

_____

_____

3 **What qualities do you think protesters needed to have in order to take part in a lunch-counter sit-in?**

_____

_____

_____

4 **What kinds of planning and organization were done ahead of time before the protesters arrived at the lunch counters?**

_____

_____

_____

Be a Reading Detective!

Return to

Harriet Tubman
Conductor
on the
UNDERGROUND
RAILROAD

"Harriet Tubman"
Student Book pp. 701–715

1 What did the author most want to show in this selection?

☐ how society has changed since the 1800s

☐ the strength and courage of Harriet Tubman

☐ how people worked together against injustice

Prove It! What evidence in the selection supports your answer? Check the boxes. ☑ Make notes.

Evidence	Notes
☐ details about Tubman's life	
☐ details about Tubman's escape	
☐ details about traveling north	

Write About It!

AUTHOR'S PURPOSE

Answer question **1** using evidence from the text.

_____

_____

_____

_____

_____

_____

_____

2 **Harriet Tubman's brothers were afraid to try to escape. What helped Tubman face the dangers?**

☐ Her faith was very strong.

☐ She refused to be on a chain gang for the rest of her life.

☐ She would rather die than be enslaved.

Prove It! What evidence in the selection supports your answer? Check the boxes. ☑ Make notes.

Evidence	Notes
☐ what Tubman says and thinks	
☐ events in Tubman's life	
☐ what others said and did	

Write About It!

CAUSE AND EFFECT

Answer question 2 using evidence from the text.

_____

_____

_____

_____

_____

_____

_____

241B

artificial
data
sensors
ultimate
uncanny

A New-Age Vacuum Cleaner

1 The Smiths' new vacuum cleaner is amazing. It has an **uncanny** ability to move around furniture without the help of a human being.

Describe a tool or a machine that you think has an <u>uncanny</u> ability to do something special.

_____

_____

_____

2 The vacuum cleaner has motion **sensors**. If they detect something that moves, like a cat, the vacuum cleaner turns away.

Imagine that you are building a flying machine. What kind of <u>sensors</u> would you put in it?

_____

_____

_____

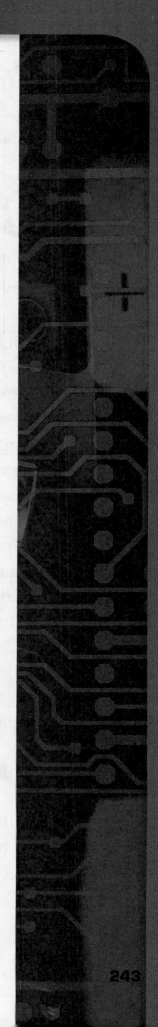

3 A computer chip in the vacuum cleaner processes **data**. Some of the information comes from the sensors. The rest comes from the Smiths, who give the machine its instructions.

Describe an experiment that you conducted. What kind of <u>data</u> did you get?

_____

_____

_____

4 The vacuum cleaner has **artificial** intelligence. It can "think" and react, but it is not alive.

Tell about something <u>artificial</u> that you know about or have seen.

_____

_____

_____

5 Ms. Smith gave the vacuum cleaner the **ultimate** test. She put it in the kids' messy playroom and turned it on.

Describe the <u>ultimate</u> model of a toy or tool you'd like to have.

_____

_____

_____

From Last to First

by John Berry

"That robot had an **uncanny** ability to get stuck in corners," said Jake. "Every time it turned around, it got stuck. Every time it threw a ball, it got stuck. Every time it moved forward or backward, it got stuck!"

Diego laughed. "I still love that robot. Sugar Ball 800. I know we're starting a new robotics season now, but she was a beauty. Remember how she nearly knocked down the principal? I thought we were doomed!"

"Thank goodness Mr. Stevens was there," said Tricia. She was talking about our team's mentor. "He explained everything. The rest of us were laughing too hard. We might have been expelled if not for Mr. Stevens."

"All SB–800 did was throw a couple of tennis balls," I said. I preferred to use the robot's formal name. "Still, I guess SB–800 did kind of run into the back of the principal's foot when it ran after the balls."

Stop Think Write

SEQUENCE OF EVENTS

Did the incident with SB-800 happen recently or a while ago? How can you tell?

_____

_____

_____

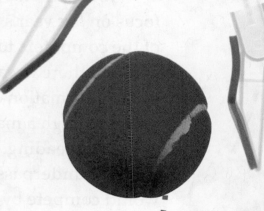

Our robotics team was meeting for the first time this year. We have fifteen members, plus Mr. Stevens, who works at an engineering company. His work focuses on <mark>artificial</mark> intelligence. He builds factory machines that see and think on their own. He's got exactly the right experience to mentor our team.

We named our team the RoboGorillas. Last year was not a good one for us. SB–800 got stuck in a corner at the regional games. Sarah was our radio operator. Usually, she could get SB–800 moving again, but this time a piece of wiring had gotten loose. SB–800 just kept bumping into the walls until time ran out. Our competitor scored about a thousand points, and we ended up with 125. Last place.

Stop Think Write

CAUSE AND EFFECT

Why did the RoboGorillas place last in the regional games last year?

_____

_____

_____

The Ball and Maze

We finally stopped talking about SB-800 so we could focus on *this* year's regional games. We logged onto one of the computers to find out the theme. I clicked onto the site, and there it was: "The Ball and Maze." According to the information on the site, each robot would have to move through a maze and collect balls of different sizes.

I kept reading. The maze would have hills, valleys, bridges, underpasses, and blind alleys. Two robots would compete by racing through the course, picking up balls, and putting them in a basket. The robots had just three minutes to complete the course. The more balls a robot retrieved, the more points the team would score.

"This will be tough on the robot's sensors," I said. I knew our robot would need to use motion and light sensors to tell different-size balls apart and to adjust movements in order to pick up the balls. I shook my head, trying to imagine all the corners where a robot could get stuck.

Stop Think Write

What will a robot's <u>sensors</u> need to detect in this competition?

_____

_____

_____

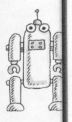

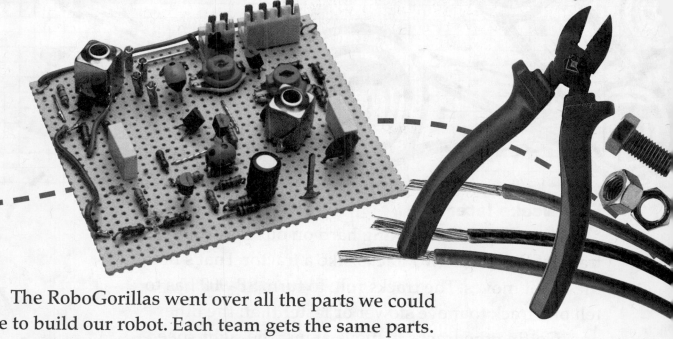

The RoboGorillas went over all the parts we could use to build our robot. Each team gets the same parts. This year there were about 400 parts.

"Listen up," said Mr. Stevens. "There have been some advances in parts since last year, which means we can build a better robot. However, we're going to have to work fast. There are just six weeks until the competition."

We spent a lot of time talking about the new central controller. The controller is like the robot's nervous system. It receives data from the sensors and the radio operator. For example, if a sensor shows that a corner is two feet away, the controller processes that information. If everything works right, the controller tells the robot's other parts what to do. Maybe the robot stops. Maybe it turns left. Maybe it turns around.

Stop   Think   Write

VOCABULARY

Explain what the central controller does with <u>data</u> it receives from a robot's sensors.

_____

_____

_____

247

Five weeks later...

Diego has been working hard on our new robot's tracks. SB-900 has two tracks, like a tractor. That's how the robot moves. The tracks roll. To turn, SB-900 has to tell one track to move slower or faster than the other one. Getting the tracks to move at just the right speed has been a challenge.

I've been helping with the programming. The central controller has to be told what to do. Programming requires speaking the controller's language. We've all been learning C++, the computer language that the controller understands.

The ultimate test is going to be the game's autonomous period. That's when each robot has to operate by itself for fifteen seconds. It can't receive any radio contact or help from its human owners, so everything needs to work perfectly.

SB–900 had a trial run today. Most parts worked well, but we still have some bugs to fix.

Stop   Think   Write

SEQUENCE OF EVENTS

What is the next thing the RoboGorillas need to do with their robot after the trial run?

_____

_____

_____

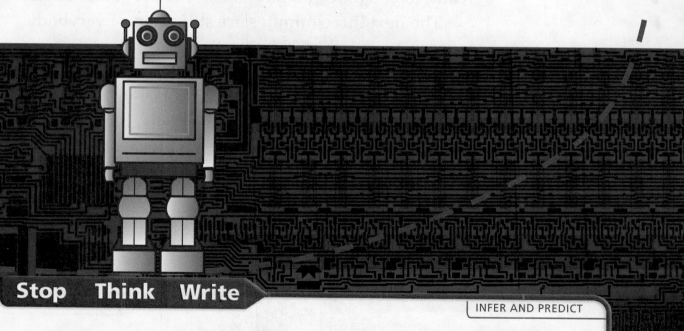

"I'm worried," Joe confided a few days later as we were walking to class.

"What are you worried about?" I asked.

"I think Sugar Ball 900 is our best robot yet. I can't believe how well it picks up those balls. Diego has it turning on a dime."

"So what's the problem?" I asked.

"I'm worried about Sarah. She seems nervous because of what happened last year. We need a cool, confident radio operator. The game is too intense for an operator with a case of nerves," said Joe.

"She'll be fine," I assured him. "Sarah understands the radio better than anyone else. She works with it every day." However, I was a little nervous, too. A couple of days ago, SB-900 had gotten stuck in a corner. Sarah had gotten it moving again in just six seconds, but she had looked flustered.

Stop Think Write

INFER AND PREDICT

Does the narrator feel absolutely confident that Sarah will be fine in the competition? How can you tell?

_____

_____

_____

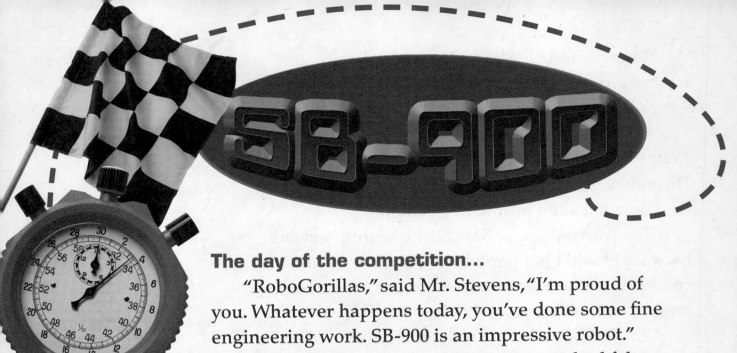

The day of the competition...

"RoboGorillas," said Mr. Stevens, "I'm proud of you. Whatever happens today, you've done some fine engineering work. SB-900 is an impressive robot."

I remembered the disappointment we had felt last year. This time, I wanted us to win. We needed to advance to the national games. Our pride was at stake.

"Team RoboGorillas, are you ready?" asked the announcer. Our handlers nodded. The other team was ready, too, so the announcer said, "Let the games begin!"

The next three minutes are still a haze. Everybody was screaming. SB-900 immediately got stuck in a corner. It felt like fate. Sarah was intense, ignoring the crowd and working the radio controls. Suddenly, SB-900 turned around and picked up two balls. Before I could blink, our robot had stuffed both balls in a basket and had picked up another, a big one.

SB-900 and the RoboGorillas kept up the good work for the rest of the competition. Believe it or not, we won! Next stop: the national games.

Stop   Think   Write

What is the first thing that happens to SB-900 at the competition?

_____

_____

_____

Look Back and Respond

1 At the first meeting of the year, what do the RoboGorillas do after they finish talking about SB-800?

Hint
For a clue, see page 246.

_____

_____

_____

2 Why is Joe worried?

Hint
For a clue, see page 249.

_____

_____

_____

3 How does SB-900's performance in this year's games compare to SB-800's performance in last year's games?

Hint
For clues, see pages 245 and 250.

_____

_____

_____

4 What comes next for Team RoboGorillas now that they have won "The Ball and Maze" contest?

Hint
For a clue, see page 250.

_____

_____

_____

Be a Reading Detective!

Return to

"Robotics"
Student Book pp. 733–745

1 In which order were the robots invented?

☐ Dante, K-bot, QRIO

☐ QRIO, K-bot, Dante

☐ K-bot, Dante, QRIO

Prove It! What evidence in the selection supports your answer?
Check the boxes. ☑ Make notes.

Evidence	Notes
☐ dates in the text	
☐ the robots' names	
☐	

Write About It!

SEQUENCE OF EVENTS

Answer question **1** using evidence from the text.

_____

_____

_____

_____

_____

_____

_____

2 Kismet doesn't really look like a person but is described as "lovable." What might give support to this opinion?

☐ details about the K-bot robot

☐ improvements in robots' vision systems

☐ Allison Bruce's research

Prove It! What evidence in the selection supports your answer? Check the boxes. ☑ Make notes.

Evidence	Notes
☐ details about people's reactions to robots	
☐ photos of robots	

Write About It!

FACT AND OPINION

Answer question **2** using evidence from the text.

_____

_____

_____

_____

_____

_____

_____

Lesson 26

TARGET VOCABULARY

impaired
innovation
miraculous
tension
void

Working in Space

People have described space as an endless **1** _____. Of course, space is not empty at all. It just seems that way because of the great distances between the planets and stars. Despite the dangers, people will always want to travel into space. In recent years, one way that people got there was the space shuttle.

In 1977, the space shuttle *Enterprise* was a new **2** _____ in space travel. That year, the *Enterprise* made many flights, but not into space. Instead, it stayed in Earth's atmosphere, for the purposes of tests and crew training.

The space shuttle *Columbia* was the first shuttle to fly in space. Imagine the excitement and

3 _____ that the crew must have felt just before the *Columbia* made its first trip, in 1981. The pilot on that first flight had never even been in space before. It must have seemed

4 _____ to pilot the shuttle into space and then return successfully to Earth.

Takeoff could sometimes damage a space shuttle. Being **5** _____ at takeoff could then endanger the flight. When the *Columbia* took off on another trip, in February of 2003, a piece of foam damaged one of its wings. Despite the problem, *Columbia* made it into space. During landing, though, the craft burst into flames and broke apart. All of the crew members were killed.

An Unearthly Job

by Richard Stull

The National Aeronautics and Space Administration (NASA) is an agency of the United States government. Astronauts train for their jobs at NASA.

In recent years, most astronauts did their work aboard a space shuttle. Many still work at the International Space Station (ISS), a huge satellite that astronauts built in space. The astronauts flew pieces of the space station into space on a shuttle. Once in space, the astronauts put the pieces together.

Astronauts still travel back and forth between Earth and the ISS. It takes about two days to reach the space station from Earth.

Stop Think Write

INFER AND PREDICT

What do you think this article will mostly be about?

_____

_____

_____

An Astronaut's Work Never Ends

At the ISS, there is a lot of work to do. Astronauts unload and check supplies brought from Earth. This requires great care. A small mistake could result in a valuable piece of equipment floating off into the void.

Sometimes astronauts have needed to repair a space shuttle or the ISS. For example, in 2007, they had to repair a damaged solar panel on the space station.

Working in space can be dangerous. Tiny pieces of rock called meteoroids zoom through space. These rocks can hit the astronauts as they work. Temperatures range from very hot to very cold, making space uncomfortable. There is also the possibility of exposure to harmful radiation from the sun.

Stop   Think   Write

MAIN IDEAS AND DETAILS

What is the main idea of the third paragraph? Give one detail that supports the main idea.

_____

_____

_____

Suiting Up for Safety

Astronauts wear space suits to protect their bodies. The suits are made of strong materials that are able to withstand the harsh conditions of space. The suits protect astronauts from extreme temperatures and from meteoroids.

The space suit has other uses, too. It has a helmet with a clear front that allows astronauts to see as they work. The suit is sealed, so astronauts can get oxygen. Each suit has a built-in radio that astronauts use to communicate with each other.

When astronauts need to move a short distance through space, they use a backpack with small rockets inside. Once their work outside is done, the astronauts return to the space station. They take off their space suits in a special chamber and put on regular clothes.

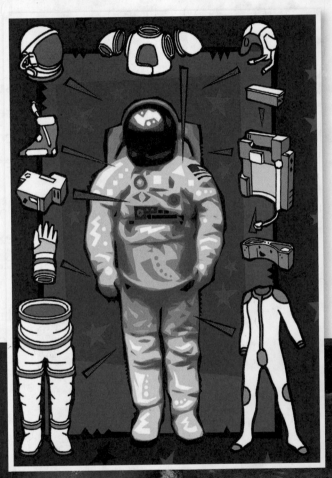

Stop   Think   Write

CAUSE AND EFFECT

Why must astronauts wear space suits?

_____

_____

_____

Living Without Gravity

Inside the ISS, astronauts don't walk—they float! That's because there is no gravity in space to hold things down. In space, people are weightless.

Astronauts have to be careful with water. A drop of floating water could jam up a computer, causing it to be permanently **impaired**. Water, crumbs, and even lint must be carefully contained at all times.

Sleeping in space is one of the easiest things to do. Astronauts can sleep anywhere because they are weightless. They can sleep upside down or float around the cabin. Some astronauts strap themselves into a sleeping bag attached to a wall. Others just fasten a pillow around their heads. Most astronauts sleep for eight hours a night.

Stop Think Write

VOCABULARY

What does the author say could cause a computer to be permanently <u>impaired</u>?

_____

_____

_____

Daily Life on the ISS

Astronauts bring food and water with them when they go into space. They store food in a kitchen on the ISS. Like most kitchens, it has a stove and a refrigerator.

Astronauts eat what most people eat, but they prepare their meals differently. Most of their food has had all water removed from it. The dried food comes sealed in packets that weigh very little and don't take up much space. To make a meal, the astronauts add water to the contents of a packet. Then they heat it up and eat the food directly from the packet.

Astronauts must dine carefully in space. That's because their food can easily float away. Just as astronauts can float across the room, so can food and utensils!

Stop   Think   Write

MAIN IDEAS AND DETAILS

Which details support the main idea that astronauts prepare food differently from people on Earth?

_____

_____

_____

Free Time in Space

Astronauts do not have much free time in space, but they do relax sometimes. They might read a book or send e-mail to a family member. They might also play an instrument or take photographs of things outside the windows. There are lots of **miraculous** sights in space!

Astronauts must exercise every day to keep their muscles strong and their bones healthy. Keeping fit and having fun help crew members avoid **tension** during space shuttle flights.

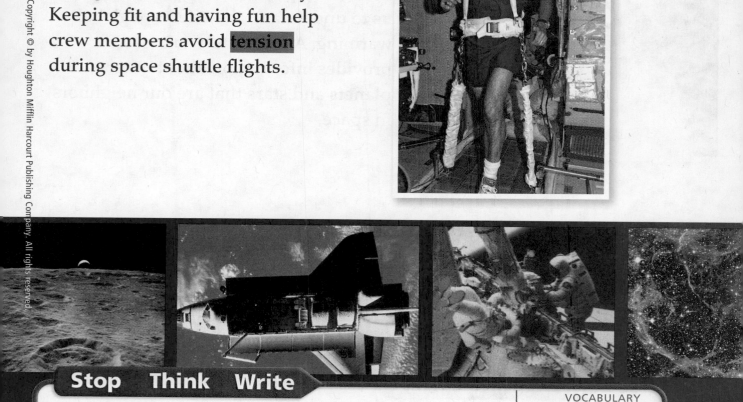

Stop Think Write

VOCABULARY

What kinds of <u>miraculous</u> sights do you think astronauts see from the space station?

_____

_____

_____

How Work in Space Helps Life on Earth

Astronauts spend most of their time in space working. Some study the effects of weightlessness or test a new computer **innovation**. Others conduct experiments, such as testing the growth of seeds in space, or the human body's reaction to being in space. Still others study what Earth looks like from space.

The work astronauts do is important to our understanding of life on Earth. For example, astronauts can measure changes in polar caps, and this helps us to understand the effects of global warming. Astronauts' work also provides information about other planets and stars that are our neighbors in space.

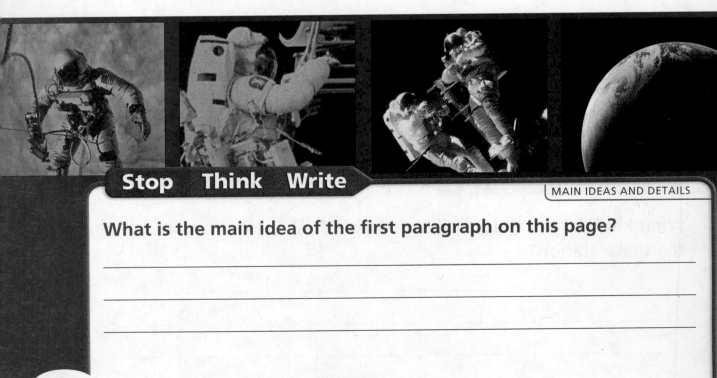

Stop Think Write

What is the main idea of the first paragraph on this page?

_____

_____

_____

Look Back and Respond

1 What is this article mainly about?

_____

_____

_____

Hint

You can find clues on almost every page.

2 How does weightlessness affect the lives of the astronauts in space?

_____

_____

_____

Hint

For clues, see pages 257, 258, and 259.

3 What details support the main idea that astronauts work hard?

_____

_____

_____

Hint

For clues, see pages 254, 255, and 260.

4 Why is the work astronauts do in space important to life on Earth?

_____

_____

_____

Hint

For clues, see page 260.

Be a Reading Detective!

Return to

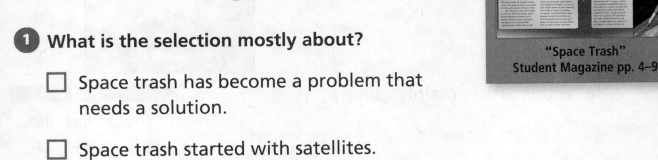

"Space Trash"
Student Magazine pp. 4–9

1 What is the selection mostly about?

☐ Space trash has become a problem that needs a solution.

☐ Space trash started with satellites.

☐ Space trash should be zapped or sent into outer space.

Prove It! What evidence in the selection supports your answer? Check the boxes. ☑ Make notes.

Evidence	Notes
☐ details about space trash dangers	
☐ photos and captions	
☐ the section "Clean Up Time!"	

Write About It!

MAIN IDEAS AND DETAILS

Answer question **1** using evidence from the text.

_____

_____

_____

_____

_____

_____

_____

2 **Why are people worried about space trash?**

☐ It could hurt someone on Earth.

☐ It could hit a spacecraft.

☐ It travels very fast.

Prove It! What evidence in the selection supports your answer? Check the boxes. ☑ Make notes.

Evidence	Notes
☐ details about spacecraft	
☐ the section "Why Worry?"	

Write About It!

CAUSE AND EFFECT

Answer question 2 using evidence from the text.

_____

_____

_____

_____

_____

_____

_____

consequences
frigid
impressive
retains
venture

Mountaintops

1 The air is **frigid** on high mountaintops during much of the year. The cold can be as extreme as that in the Arctic.

Describe the most frigid place you have visited.

_____

_____

_____

2 Winds can reach very **impressive** speeds on mountaintops. In a 1934 storm, wind gusted over New Hampshire's Mt. Washington at 231 miles per hour!

What impressive weather event have you witnessed?

_____

_____

_____

3 A high mountain peak **retains** its original wildlife. Few people visit, so plants and animals aren't disturbed.

Describe something that retains its shape after you use it.

_____

_____

_____

4 Many mountains have glaciers, which are giant rivers of ice. One of the consequences of global warming is the melting of glaciers.

What are the consequences of a big storm?

_____

_____

_____

5 Few people will venture to the peaks of the world's tallest mountains. The dangers at such heights are too great for most of us.

What is something that you would venture to do?

_____

_____

_____

The Arctic: A Melting Ocean

by John Berry

Imagine walking on top of an ocean. Believe it or not, there is an ocean you can walk on! It is the Arctic Ocean. Sadly, we may not be able to walk on it in the future.

The Arctic Ocean surrounds the North Pole. It is the world's smallest ocean. Thick ice covers most of the Arctic Ocean. In some places, the ice is twenty feet thick or more.

Scientists who study this unusual ocean observe animals that live on top of and below the ice. They also study the ice itself. They measure and drill, taking samples from deep within.

Scientists have discovered that the ice cover is changing. There is less of it than there used to be. Scientists believe this may be one of the **consequences** of global warming.

Stop Think Write

CONCLUSIONS AND GENERALIZATIONS

What conclusion have scientists drawn about why ice in the Arctic Ocean is thinning?

_____

_____

_____

The Ice Zone

The Arctic Ocean has two parts: the ice zone and the water zone. The ice zone consists of frozen seawater, snowdrifts, and ridges and walls of ice. There are even mountains of ice.

Despite the intense cold, many animals live in the ice zone, including hares, polar bears, birds, and seals. These animals have learned how to live on the ice.

There is life within the ice, too. Tiny one-cell plants live deep in the ice. They are so small that you can see them only with a microscope.

The ice zone isn't always the same size. It changes during the year. In the summer, when the air heats up, the water below the ice becomes warmer. As a result, pools of water form on the surface of the ice, cracks appear, and some of the ice splits apart.

Stop Think Write

CAUSE AND EFFECT

What causes pools of water to form on the surface of the ice?

_____

_____

_____

A Freezing Cold Sea

The Arctic Ocean goes down 4,000 feet in some places. That may sound deep, but the Arctic is actually the shallowest ocean on Earth.

The Arctic's frigid water stays within a few degrees of freezing. Divers say that the water feels thicker than normal seawater. That's because it's almost frozen. If you were to stick just one finger in the Arctic, you'd jump back from the cold.

Surprisingly, many creatures live in the Arctic Ocean. Some fish thrive here, such as the Arctic cod. You can also find crabs, starfish, and sea cucumbers crawling along the ocean floor.

Some whales live in the Arctic Ocean, too, including the narwhal. Nicknamed the "unicorn of the sea," the male narwhal has a single tusk on the front of its head that can grow to an impressive length— sometimes over nine feet!

Stop Think Write

CONCLUSIONS AND GENERALIZATIONS

Why is it surprising that many creatures live in the Arctic Ocean?

_____

_____

_____

A Changing Sea

Canadian scientist Roy Koerner spent time studying the Arctic Ocean and walking on its ice. In 1969, he made the ultimate trip. He and three others were brave enough to **venture** all the way across the Arctic Ocean on dogsleds.

Koerner's trip would not be possible today. That's because the ocean has changed. The water zone is growing, while the ice zone is shrinking. There is less ice now than at any time since people began keeping records. In some places, the ice is half as thick as it used to be.

Some say the changes are due to global warming. Global warming affects many places. However, scientists claim it's happening as much as seven times faster in the Arctic than in other areas. Much has changed since Koerner began his study of the Arctic. He once described today's Arctic Ocean as "a different world."

The Past

The Present

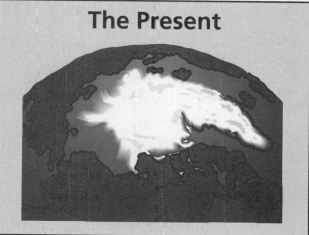

The Future

Stop Think Write

VOCABULARY

Why did it take bravery to <u>venture</u> across the Arctic Ocean?

_____

_____

_____

A Quickly Melting Ocean

Sunlight bounces off ice, but ocean water absorbs light. The water **retains** the heat from sunlight. The more open water, the more heat the ocean captures. The warmer the ocean gets, the more the ice melts, causing the water to soak up even more sunlight. The cycle continues.

Melting ice is a big problem for animals living in the ice zone. For example, polar bears have adapted to life on the ice. Layers of blubber keep them warm, pads on their feet keep them from slipping on ice, and their white color helps them blend in. Polar bears aren't just suited for the ice—they need it. They use ice for hunting. They wait next to holes in the ice for seals to come up for air. When a seal comes up, a polar bear catches its meal. Without the ice, hunting is almost impossible. According to scientists, polar bears may be extinct within a hundred years.

Stop   Think   Write

VOCABULARY

What happens when open water in the Arctic <u>retains</u> the sun's heat?

_____

_____

_____

Effects on People

Melting ice affects more than just animals in the Arctic. It affects people, too. Many people live near the ocean's edge. Ice near the shore protects their villages by stopping the waves from coming ashore during storms.

The shrinking ice is a threat to villages. Waves wear down the shorelines and cause the ground to fall into the sea. Over time, the ocean moves inland. In some villages, the sea is turning homes into debris. When the shoreline crumbles, homes along its edge crash into the water.

For people living in the Arctic, the melting ocean is a terrible problem. Many have to leave the villages that their ancestors built and start over somewhere else.

Stop Think Write

CAUSE AND EFFECT

How does the loss of ice affect Arctic villages?

_____

_____

_____

Adapting to Change

Despite the damage caused by melting ice, the people of the Arctic are making the best of climate change. For example, more areas of open water make it easier to fish. Open water also makes travel and shipping easier and quicker.

Long ago, explorers and merchants dreamed of a Northwest Passage through the Arctic Ocean. They thought the passage would begin in the Atlantic Ocean, go through the Arctic, and end at the Pacific Ocean. The dream has never come true because ice has always blocked the way. Soon, however, this may change.

Scientists do not know exactly what will happen to the Arctic Ocean. One thing is certain, though. Scientists following in the footsteps of Roy Koerner will be keeping a close watch on this changing sea.

Stop   Think   Write

CONCLUSIONS AND GENERALIZATIONS

How could the dream of a Northwest Passage finally become a reality?

_____

_____

_____

Look Back and Respond

1 Scientist Roy Koerner concluded that the Arctic Ocean is "a different world" today. What evidence supports his conclusion?

_____

_____

_____

Hint

For a clue, see page 267.

2 Overall, would an ice-free Arctic Ocean be good for animals that live in the ice zone? Explain.

_____

_____

_____

Hint

For a clue, see page 268.

3 What general statement can you make about the effects of the melting ocean on the people who live in the Arctic?

_____

_____

_____

Hint

For a clue, see page 269.

4 How could global warming help fishermen?

_____

_____

_____

Hint

For a clue, see page 270.

Be a Reading Detective!

Return to

"Denali Dog Sled Journal"
Student Magazine pp. 18–25

1 Which is true, based on the selection?

☐ Earthquakes and moose are the park's greatest dangers.

☐ The park is too cold to support life.

☐ Animals and plants can survive even on the permafrost.

Prove It! What evidence in the selection supports your answer?
Check the boxes. ☑ Make notes.

Evidence	Notes
☐ details about animals	
☐ details about plants	
☐ details about weather	

Write About It!

CONCLUSIONS AND GENERALIZATIONS

Answer question **1** using evidence from the text.

_____

_____

_____

_____

_____

_____

2 **What is the selection mostly about?**

☐ In the winter, sled dogs need extra fats and vitamins to do their work in Denali National Park.

☐ A Denali National Park ranger does not know what will happen from one day to the next.

☐ Snowshoeing in Alaska can be dangerous.

Prove It! What evidence in the selection supports your answer? Check the boxes. ☑ Make notes.

Evidence	Notes
☐ the headings	
☐ things the ranger does	
☐	

Write About It!

MAIN IDEAS AND DETAILS

Answer question **2** using evidence from the text.

_____

_____

_____

_____

_____

_____

_____

affirmed
deduced
distinguish
motive
perilous

Butterfly Watching

1 Observing some animals in nature can be **perilous**. Luckily, butterfly watching is not. It is both fun and safe to observe butterflies in their natural habitat.

Describe a perilous animal-watching situation.

_____

_____

_____

2 There are more butterflies in Texas than anywhere else in the United States. You can see many different types at the International Butterfly Park in the Rio Grande Valley. One **motive** for creating the park was to teach people about butterflies.

What motive could a visitor have to visit the International Butterfly Park?

_____

_____

3 One butterfly watcher noticed every detail of the butterflies she observed. By paying attention to details, she was able to **distinguish** one butterfly from another.

Think about bird watching, another popular hobby. Besides each bird's physical appearance, what helps you <u>distinguish</u> one bird from another?

_____

_____

_____

4 The butterfly watcher came upon a large orange butterfly with black markings. Based on what she remembered about butterflies, she **deduced** that it was a monarch butterfly.

Write a synonym for <u>deduced</u>.

_____

5 The butterfly watcher looked at her guidebook and found a picture of the butterfly she was observing. She **affirmed** that it was indeed a monarch butterfly.

What did the butterfly watcher see that <u>affirmed</u> her identification of the monarch?

_____

_____

_____

Jay's Butterflies

by Margaret Maugenest

Jay Jackson and Mattie Helm sit next to each other in class. Jay is enthusiastic about butterflies. He takes his butterfly field guide with him everywhere he goes.

"Why are you always lugging that book around?" asked Mattie one day.

"I like to study the pictures," he answered. "That way, when I see a butterfly, I know what kind it is."

Mattie rolled her eyes and made a yawning motion with her hand over her mouth. "I can't think of anything more BO-RING!"

Jay shrugged his shoulders. "Well, you'd be surprised by how many different butterflies there are around here," he told her. He would have told her more, but Mattie wasn't really listening. She was busy sending a text message to her friend Sally about where to meet after school.

Stop Think Write

UNDERSTANDING CHARACTERS

How does Mattie feel about Jay's hobby? How can you tell?

_____

_____

_____

The following day was Saturday, and Jay did what he always did on the weekend. He packed up his field guide, binoculars, notepad, camera, water, a protein bar, and an apple. The digital camera was a birthday gift from his Aunt Lucy. The zoom lens was great for taking close-up photos of butterflies and other creatures.

"What are you hoping to find today?" his mom asked. She knew where he was going.

"I really hope I see a swallowtail," said Jay on his way out the door.

"Good luck!" she called after him. She was happy to know that her son was spending time outdoors in the fresh air.

Stop Think Write

UNDERSTANDING CHARACTERS

What is Jay like? How can you tell?

_____

_____

_____

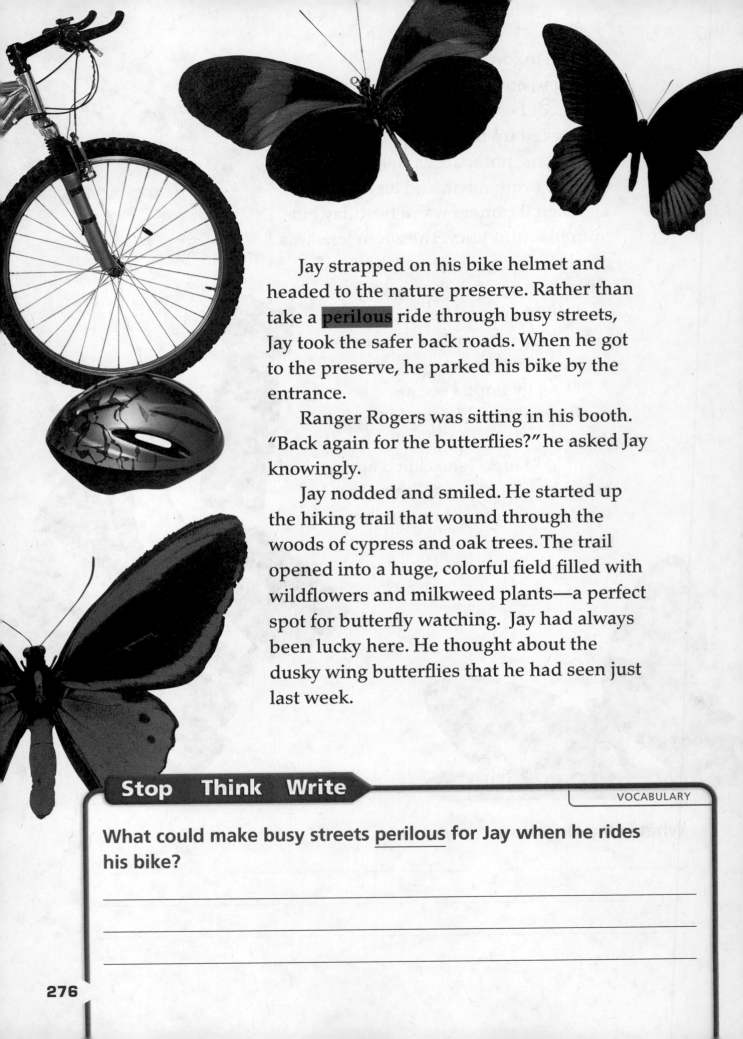

Jay strapped on his bike helmet and headed to the nature preserve. Rather than take a perilous ride through busy streets, Jay took the safer back roads. When he got to the preserve, he parked his bike by the entrance.

Ranger Rogers was sitting in his booth. "Back again for the butterflies?" he asked Jay knowingly.

Jay nodded and smiled. He started up the hiking trail that wound through the woods of cypress and oak trees. The trail opened into a huge, colorful field filled with wildflowers and milkweed plants—a perfect spot for butterfly watching. Jay had always been lucky here. He thought about the dusky wing butterflies that he had seen just last week.

Stop   Think   Write

VOCABULARY

What could make busy streets perilous for Jay when he rides his bike?

_____

_____

_____

Jay breathed in the fresh air. He looked up at the clear blue sky and felt the warm sun shining down. A gentle breeze rustled through the grasses and plants.

Watching butterflies took time and patience, but Jay liked that about his hobby. Spending time in nature was one motive Jay had for watching butterflies. Looking for interesting butterflies was also like a treasure hunt. His treasure was seeing a butterfly, looking at it closely to distinguish its shape, color, and markings, and finally identifying it. He usually tried to take some pictures. Jay was proud of his collection of butterfly photographs.

He took out his binoculars and camera and put them around his neck for quick and easy access. He listened to two songbirds twittering and watched them flit from tree to tree. Jay observed the birds through his binoculars and then scanned the field to see what insects were hovering nearby.

Stop   Think   Write

VOCABULARY

What is Jay's <u>motive</u> for pulling out his binoculars?

_____

_____

_____

Through his binoculars, Jay spotted multicolored shapes fluttering over a bush. He adjusted the focus for a better look and then smiled. They were definitely butterflies.

As Jay walked in their direction, he came upon two black and yellow butterflies dancing in the breeze. Jay kept his eyes on them while pulling out his camera. When one butterfly landed on a flower, Jay sneaked up to it. He moved as quietly as possible and snapped a picture. Then he zoomed in on the butterfly to get a shot of it sucking up the sweet nectar inside the flower. Its striped wings were folded.

Jay felt his excitement mounting when he noticed the tail shape at the end of the butterfly's wings. From the markings and the tail, he **deduced** that it was a tiger swallowtail.

Jay held his breath. He hoped that he could get a clear photograph. He waited for the exact moment. Just as the butterfly opened its wings, Jay clicked the camera. He got the shot he wanted!

Stop Think Write

How can you tell that Jay is a good photographer?

_____

_____

_____

Back at home, Jay downloaded the pictures from his camera to his laptop. He didn't like to capture butterflies and mount them, because that meant the butterflies would die. Taking photos caused no harm to the butterflies.

Comparing his photographs of the tiger swallowtail with the pictures in the field guide, Jay affirmed that his find was indeed a swallowtail. He was very excited. It was exactly the butterfly he'd been hoping to see! He showed his parents the photo.

"You said you hoped you would see a swallowtail, and you did!" said his mom. "I'm happy for you."

"Yep, me too," said his dad. "Life's like that, Jay. Sometimes you get lucky!"

Stop Think Write

CONCLUSIONS AND GENERALIZATIONS

How is Jay's way of butterfly collecting better than capturing real butterflies?

_____

_____

_____

Jay thought about Mattie, specifically about how she had told him that butterfly watching was boring. "I'll show her," he thought. He printed out a photograph just for her, and he put it in an envelope.

On Monday, Jay handed the envelope to Mattie just as she got to her desk. "See what I found over the weekend," he said proudly.

Mattie took the envelope. "For me?" she asked, opening it. Jay watched her. He couldn't help but notice her eyes light up and a little smile come over her face.

"You took this picture?" she asked.

"Who else?" he answered.

"Not bad. Thanks," she said. Then she carefully put the picture back in the envelope and placed it in her desk.

Stop   Think   Write

UNDERSTANDING CHARACTERS

Why do you think Jay gives Mattie the picture?

_____

_____

_____

Look Back and Respond

1 **How can you tell that Jay doesn't mind doing things by himself?**

_____

_____

_____

Hint

Clues you can use are on almost every page!

2 **Give three examples in the story that show how Jay is observant, or looks at things carefully.**

_____

_____

_____

Hint

For clues, see pages 277, 278, and 279.

3 **How do Jay's parents feel about his butterfly watching?**

_____

_____

_____

Hint

For clues, see pages 275 and 279.

4 **Do you think Mattie changes her mind about butterflies? Explain.**

_____

_____

_____

Hint

For clues, see pages 274 and 280.

Be a Reading Detective!

Return to

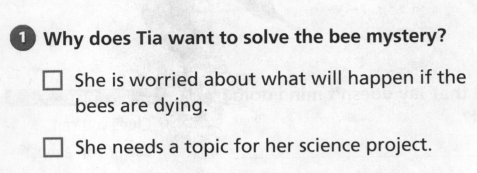

"Vanishing Act"
Student Magazine pp. 34–41

1 **Why does Tia want to solve the bee mystery?**

☐ She is worried about what will happen if the bees are dying.

☐ She needs a topic for her science project.

☐ Both of the above answers are correct.

Prove It! What evidence in the story supports your answer?
Check the boxes. ☑ Make notes.

Evidence	Notes
☐ how farmers use bees	
☐ what Tia says to Justin	
☐ things we use that come from bees	

Write About It!

UNDERSTANDING CHARACTERS

Answer question **1** using evidence from the text.

_____

_____

_____

_____

_____

_____

_____

2 **Which of these statements is true, based on the selection?**

☐ Cell phone towers endanger honeybees.

☐ Changes to the environment endanger animals.

☐ A lot of our food depends on bees.

Prove It! What evidence in the story supports your answer?
Check the boxes. ☑ Make notes.

Evidence	Notes
☐ things Tia learns from her research on the honeybee mystery	
☐ the specific topic of Tia's science project	

Write About It!

Answer question ② using evidence from the text.

_____

_____

_____

_____

_____

_____

destiny
embrace
majestic
massive
temperaments

About Whales

Whales are beautiful, majestic mammals that live in the sea. Some are massive. For example, the blue whale can grow to be over 90 feet long and over 150 tons. That's as big as a nine-story building. In fact, the blue whale is the largest animal on Earth.

Despite their huge size, whales are difficult to spot. If you should see one, embrace the moment. Sadly, the destiny of these amazing creatures does not look good. The humpback whale is just one of several species in danger of becoming extinct.

Legends describe whales as gentle giants. For example, even though orcas are called "killer whales," their temperaments are not very aggressive.

1 Some whales are small, but most are

_____.

2 If you see a humpback whale,

_____ the moment, as these are

endangered animals.

3 Surprisingly, killer whales do not have very

aggressive _____.

4 What is the most majestic sight you have ever
seen? What made it so special?

_____

_____

_____

5 Why might endangered animals have a sad
destiny?

_____

_____

_____

Giants of the Sea

by Mia Lewis

Whales are among the most fascinating and amazing creatures on the planet. Their majestic size, grace, and intelligence set them apart from other animals. Don't pass up a chance to see whales for yourself.

Whale watching requires great patience. You will see more waves than whales, and you may spend most of the time scanning the horizon. However, the moment you spot your first whale, you'll feel that all the hours of searching were worth it.

Whales do the most amazing things. They "spy-hop," resting vertically while popping their heads up above the water to look around. They "lob-tail," lifting their enormous tails into the air and bringing them down with a loud splat. They "breach," jumping right out of the water. Watching whales perform is a show you do not want to miss.

Stop Think Write

PERSUASION

How does the author try to persuade readers to see whales for themselves?

_____

_____

_____

Whales Breathe and Birth Like Humans

Whales may live in the sea, but they are mammals, like humans. Whales breathe into their lungs, just as we do, coming to the surface from time to time to get air. Not many mammals live in the sea. Whales are unusual in this way.

Instead of having a nose with nostrils, a whale has a blowhole at the top of its head. When the blowhole appears above the surface of the water, a fountain of water may shoot high into the sky.

Whales give birth to live young, like other mammals. They have just one baby, or calf, at a time. The calf can swim as soon as it is born in order to keep up with its mother. The mother nurses the calf with rich milk, which is high in fat content, to keep her baby warm in the cold waters.

Like other mammals, whales are warm-blooded. Even without hair or fur, they maintain a steady body temperature. A thick layer of fat right under the skin, called blubber, helps whales maintain their body heat.

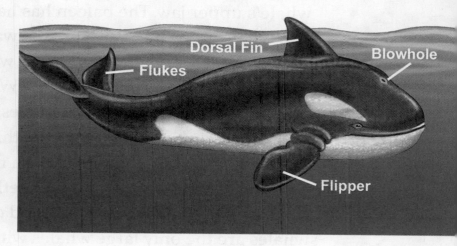

Dorsal Fin

Blowhole

Flukes

Flipper

Stop Think Write

COMPARE AND CONTRAST

How are whales like humans? How are they different?

_____

_____

_____

A baleen whale

A toothed whale

Not All Whales Are the Same

There are seventy-six species of whales, and they can be divided into two main groups: *baleen* and *toothed*. The biggest whales are baleen. Surprisingly, these massive creatures have no teeth!

Instead of teeth, baleen whales have baleen plates that work like strainers. Baleen is a hard but elastic substance that looks like a comb hanging from the whale's upper jaw. The baleen has hairy bristles. The whale gulps huge amounts of water as it swims near the surface. Then it forces the water out of its mouth, through the baleen plates. When small food organisms are caught on the bristles, the whale uses its tongue to guide them down its throat. It takes a lot of straining and slurping to make a meal!

Most whales, however, have teeth and are smaller. Killer whales (which are also called orcas) and sperm whales are the only large whales with teeth.

Stop Think Write

INFER AND PREDICT

Why does the author find it surprising that baleen whales have no teeth?

_____

_____

_____

286

Whales on Show

Some whales live in captivity in marine parks, where they perform in shows. Killer whales are among the most popular attractions.

Skilled trainers work with the mammals to teach them "tricks." Killer whales' even and acrobatic temperaments make them well suited to participate in marine park shows. However, a whale is still an animal and therefore unpredictable. As much as you may want to embrace a whale, it is dangerous for anyone but a trainer to make contact.

The shows are fun, but some people disapprove of them because the whales in shows are captive. These people feel that no matter how good the conditions are, it is not fair to keep a whale out of its natural habitat. Whales were born to be free.

Stop Think Write

VOCABULARY

Why could it be dangerous to <u>embrace</u> a whale?

_____

_____

_____

Whale
hunters at work

Whale Hunting

For thousands of years, people have hunted whales for everything from meat for food to oil for lamps. Whale hunting, or whaling, has been a terrible threat to the world's whales. Hunters killed so many whales during the first half of the 20th century that today many species are close to extinct.

The International Whaling Commission (IWC) banned most commercial whaling in 1986. However, some native peoples have permission to kill a specific number of whales each year to help preserve their traditional cultures.

Not all countries are members of the IWC. Some non-member countries continue to hunt whales. They say that a controlled amount of whaling is safe. However, only a complete ban will stop the cruelty to these magnificent creatures.

Stop   Think   Write

PERSUASION

How do you think the author wants the reader to feel about whaling? How can you tell?

_____

_____

_____

Helping Whales

Despite the general ban on whaling, whales are still in danger. Accidents cause more whale deaths than hunting. Ships, for example, accidentally kill many whales each year. There should be laws to make ships slow down in areas where whales live and travel.

Hitting whales with ships is just one way that humans harm these wonderful creatures. Many whales also die getting tangled in nets set out by fishermen. Pollution, climate change, and too much noise are bad for whales, too.

The destiny of whales is in our hands. We must work to find solutions to the problems that threaten these amazing animals. If we don't, many species of whales may become extinct. Once a species of whale is extinct, it is gone forever. It is sad to think of a world without whales.

Stop Think Write

PERSUASION

How does the author try to persuade the reader that it is important to protect whales?

_____

_____

_____

Whale

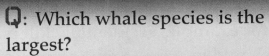

Q&A

Q: Which whale species is the largest?

A: The largest whale is the blue whale. It can grow to over 90 feet long and weigh over 150 tons! Blue whales are an endangered species.

Q: Which whale travels farthest?

A: Gray whales migrate as far as 12,500 miles each year. In the summer, they feed in the cold Arctic waters. They give birth to their young in the warm waters off Baja California. They often travel close to the coast. Thousands of people go to see them pass by in the spring and fall.

Q: Which whale is most at risk of becoming extinct?

A: The northern right whale is the most endangered of all whales. It lives along the Atlantic coast of North America. Only about 350 of these whales remain.

Stop Think Write

AUTHOR'S PURPOSE

Why do you think the author gives information about blue whales and northern right whales being endangered?

_____

_____

_____

Look Back and Respond

1 **What are the two main groups of whales? Which group do most whales belong to?**

Hint

Look for clues on page 286.

_____

_____

_____

2 **What argument does the author use to persuade the reader that it is cruel to keep whales in marine parks?**

Hint

For a clue, see page 287.

_____

_____

3 **Why does the IWC allow some native groups to hunt some whales each year?**

Hint

For a clue, see page 288.

_____

_____

_____

4 **Write two details about gray whales that you can find in this article.**

Hint

For clues, see page 290.

_____

_____

_____

Be a Reading Detective!

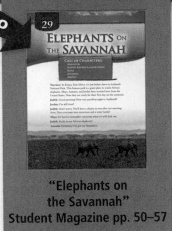

Return to

"Elephants on
the Savannah"
Student Magazine pp. 50–57

1 **What is the author's opinion?**

☐ that national parks are educational

☐ that elephants are intelligent, amazing animals

☐ both of the above

Prove It! What evidence in the play supports your answer?
Check the boxes. ☑ Make notes.

Evidence	Notes
☐ what the three friends see in the park	
☐ what the narrator says about the park	
☐ what the ranger says about elephants	

Write About It!

PERSUASION

Answer question 1 using evidence from the text.

_____

_____

_____

_____

_____

_____

_____

2 **What do the friends learn about the elephant bones?**

☐ The elephant was young.

☐ Elephants mourn their dead.

☐ Elephants carry bones with them on long journeys.

Prove It! What evidence in the play supports your answer?
Check the boxes. ☑ Make notes.

Evidence	Notes
☐ things the elephants do	
☐ things Judith says	

Write About It!

MAIN IDEAS AND DETAILS

Answer question ② using evidence from the text.

_____

_____

_____

_____

_____

_____

**conditions
data
intently
jeopardy
subsided**

Hurricane Danger

1 During a hurricane, weather **conditions** become very dangerous. High winds and floods damage property and threaten human life.

How might hurricane <u>conditions</u> be dangerous to a person?

_____

_____

_____

2 Weather forecasters track hurricanes. They collect **data** about a storm's speed and location. These facts help forecasters decide if a hurricane is dangerous.

What tools might scientists use to collect <u>data</u> about a hurricane?

_____

_____

_____

3 When a hurricane approaches, forecasters follow it **intently**. They watch closely to learn its path and predict where it will land.

When might you need to follow events intently?

_____

_____

_____

4 A hurricane can place an entire city in **jeopardy**. Forecasters must warn people about approaching storms so that they can get out of harm's way.

If you were in jeopardy from an approaching storm, what would you do?

_____

_____

_____

5 After a bad hurricane, when the winds and high water have **subsided**, the cleanup begins. People work hard to get their homes, and their lives, back in order again.

Why must people wait until winds have subsided before they can clean up?

_____

_____

_____

The Worst Hurricane Ever

by Duncan Searl

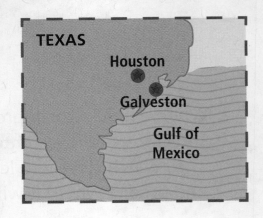

TEXAS
Houston
Galveston
Gulf of Mexico

In 1900, the city of Galveston was booming. With a population of 42,000, it was the largest city in Texas. Galveston boasted electric lights, streetcars, concert halls, luxury hotels, and long-distance telephones.

Trade made the city rich. Ships from around the world docked at Galveston Bay, a natural harbor. The location, however, made some people nervous. Since Galveston sat on a low island in the bay, they wanted to build a seawall to protect the city from hurricanes.

The United States Weather Bureau thought that a seawall was not necessary. Officials assured the people of Galveston that there was nothing to worry about.

Scientists believed that the floor of the Gulf of Mexico, which slopes gradually away from Galveston, would stop hurricanes from forming there. Today we know this is not true.

Stop Think Write

TEXT AND GRAPHIC FEATURES

Look at the map. How does Galveston's location make the city vulnerable to hurricanes?

_____

_____

_____

294

A Reason to Worry

On September 8, 1900, the people of Galveston awoke to a surprising sight: several inches of water running down their streets. What they saw wasn't rain—it was seawater!

Children splashed in the water and sailed toy boats. Crowds walked down to the beach. High waves crashed against the seafront shops.

Everyone knew a storm was coming, but people were not worried. Storms were fairly common, and most did not cause much damage.

However, on the Gulf of Mexico, the captain of the *Pensacola* was worried. He had just sailed out of Galveston into a terrible hurricane. High waves crashed over his steamship, and 120-mile-per-hour winds tore away the anchor.

The hurricane was heading straight for Galveston, but the captain had no way of warning the city. Ship radios were a new invention, and the *Pensacola* didn't have one.

Stop Think Write

TEXT AND GRAPHIC FEATURES

Look at the head "A Reason to Worry." How does it hint at the effect the hurricane will have on Galveston?

_____

_____

_____

Conditions Worsen

Weather forecasters in Cuba were worried, too. A storm passed over that island on September 4. The forecasters watched it **intently** and reported that the storm was curving into the Gulf of Mexico.

Weather officials in Washington, D.C., got the report from Cuba, but they didn't believe it. They thought the storm was moving up the Atlantic coast. Remember, storm forecasting was a new science in 1900. With no satellites or airplanes, collecting **data** on hurricanes was difficult. There was no radar, either, making it impossible to track storms closely.

The officials didn't want to make a mistake. A false hurricane warning was costly and embarrassing, so officials posted no warnings for the Gulf of Mexico.

Meanwhile, people in Galveston watched nervously as the water continued to rise.

Stop Think Write

CAUSE AND EFFECT

Why didn't weather officials give hurricane warnings for the Gulf of Mexico?

_____

_____

_____

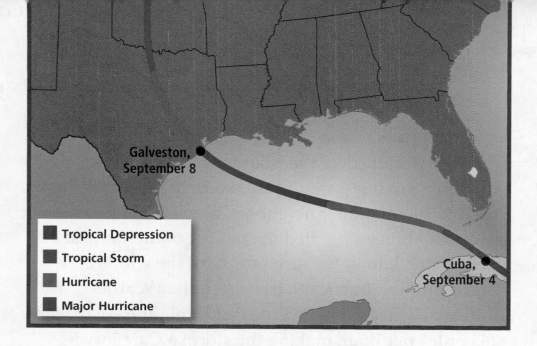

Tropical Depression

Tropical Storm

Hurricane

Major Hurricane

Disaster Strikes!

Conditions on the island of Galveston worsened. The water rose steadily, the winds picked up, and a heavy rain began.

Wind tore down the telegraph and telephone lines, cutting off communication with the mainland. No one outside Galveston knew what was happening. Railroad lines from the city were soon underwater, making it impossible to leave. There was no escape.

The Weather Service used special flags for hurricane warnings. Officials never raised those flags in Galveston, though. Most people still thought they would be safe at home. Only a few went to schools and churches for safety.

At 7:30 P.M. on September 8, the hurricane made landfall. It was a direct hit on Galveston.

Stop Think Write

TEXT AND GRAPHIC FEATURES

How does the map on this page help you understand the power of the hurricane that hit Galveston?

_____

_____

_____

No One Is Safe

A wall of water—the storm surge—swept across the island. In just a few seconds, water inside houses rose four feet. Eventually, twenty feet of water would cover the island.

People in one-story houses were in **jeopardy**. Many tried to swim to their neighbors' larger homes. People in two-story houses hurried upstairs or to their attics.

No one knows for sure how hard the winds blew that night. The hurricane destroyed the Weather Bureau's instruments. Wind speeds might have reached 165 miles per hour, making the storm a Category 5 hurricane, the most dangerous and destructive kind.

The buildings along the Gulf Coast fell first. In the high winds, shingles and boards became missiles. Even telephone poles flew through the air. No one was safe from the flying objects.

Stop Think Write

Describe two ways in which the people of Galveston were in jeopardy.

_____

_____

_____

The Damage

A mountain of wreckage formed near the beach. Pushed by winds and water, debris moved across the island. As the wreckage moved, it grew. Like a giant bulldozer, it leveled much of Galveston.

The side of the island facing the Gulf of Mexico suffered most. Even the strongest houses there could not stand up to the winds and water. Eventually, the houses broke apart.

Terrified families floated off with their houses. People clung to doors, walls, and roofs. In the rain and darkness, they had no idea where they were. Their neighborhoods were gone. Galveston was now part of the Gulf of Mexico.

Finally, during the night, the winds subsided. The water slowly flowed back into the sea.

Damaged homes and debris after a hurricane.

Stop Think Write

VOCABULARY

How do you think the survivors felt when the winds finally subsided?

_____

_____

_____

299

The Aftermath

When the sun rose the next day, survivors couldn't believe their eyes. The hurricane had destroyed 3,600 buildings. A tangled mass of broken boards, furniture, and personal belongings covered much of the island.

The deadly hurricane killed at least 7,000 people, making it the worst natural disaster in U.S. history.

In the years that followed, the people of Galveston rebuilt their city. Soon, there were new railroads, concert halls, and luxury hotels. The pride of Galveston, however, was its new seventeen-foot seawall.

Since 1900, the seawall has protected the city from many hurricanes. In addition, modern technology now lets scientists track storms more accurately. They can alert cities to hurricanes days in advance so that people have time to move to safety. When Hurricane Ike struck Galveston in 2008, the damage, though severe, was nothing like the terrible losses of 1900.

Stop Think Write

MAIN IDEAS AND DETAILS

After the 1900 hurricane, what did the people of Galveston do to protect their city from future storms?

_____

_____

_____

Look Back and Respond

1 Think about the title of this article. What does it tell you about the Galveston hurricane of 1900?

_____

_____

_____

Hint

Clues you can use are on pages 298, 299, and 300.

2 How does the photograph on page 299 help you understand what hurricanes can do?

_____

_____

_____

Hint

What do you see in the photograph?

3 Do you think the job of rebuilding Galveston after the 1900 hurricane was easy, somewhat difficult, or very difficult? Explain.

_____

_____

_____

Hint

Clues you can use are on page 300.

4 How are people better able to prepare for hurricanes today than they were in 1900?

_____

_____

_____

Hint

Clues you can use are on pages 296 and 300.

Be a Reading Detective!

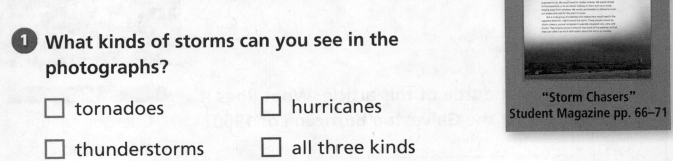

"Storm Chasers"
Student Magazine pp. 66–71

1 What kinds of storms can you see in the photographs?

☐ tornadoes   ☐ hurricanes

☐ thunderstorms   ☐ all three kinds

Prove It! What evidence in the selection supports your answer?
Check the boxes. ☑   Make notes.

Evidence	Notes
☐ the photographs	
☐ the captions	
☐ the text that describes storms	

Write About It!

TEXT AND GRAPHIC FEATURES

Answer question **1** using evidence from the text.

_____

_____

_____

_____

_____

_____

_____

2 **What advice does the author give for staying safe during a storm?**

☐ Become a storm chaser.

☐ Seek shelter indoors.

☐ Sometimes storms are not dangerous.

Prove It! What evidence in the selection supports your answer? Check the boxes. ☑ Make notes.

Evidence	Notes
☐ descriptions of storms	
☐ advice for "most of us"	
☐ dangers that storm chasers face	

Write About It!

AUTHOR'S PURPOSE

Answer question **2** using evidence from the text.

_____

_____

_____

_____

_____

_____

Summarize Strategy

When you **summarize**, briefly retell the important ideas in a text.

- Use your own words.

- Organize ideas in a way that makes sense.

- Do not change the meaning of the text.

- Make your summary short. Use only a few sentences.

When you **paraphrase**, restate the author's words in a new way. A paraphrase can be about as long as the text.

- Use synonyms.

- Change the order of words in a sentence.

- Combine sentences. Put related ideas together.

Analyze/Evaluate Strategy

You can **analyze** and **evaluate** a text. Study the text carefully. Then form an opinion about it.

1. Analyze the text. Look at the ideas. Think about what the author tells you.
   - What are the important facts and details?
   - How are the ideas organized?
   - What does the author want you to know?

2. Evaluate the text. Decide what is important. Then form an opinion.
   - How do you feel about what you read?
   - Do you agree with the author's ideas?
   - Did the author succeed in reaching his or her goals?

Infer/Predict Strategy

You can make an **inference**. Figure out what the author does not tell you.

- Think about the clues in the text.

- Think about what you already know.

You can make a **prediction**. Use text clues to figure out what will happen next.

Monitor/Clarify Strategy

You can **monitor** what you read. Pay attention to how well you understand the text.

If you read a part that doesn't make sense, find a way to **clarify** it. Clear up what you don't understand.

- Use what you already know.

- Reread or read ahead. Find clues in the text.

- Read more slowly.

- Ask questions about the text.

Question Strategy

Ask yourself **questions** before, during, and after you read. Look for answers.

Some questions to ask:
- What does the author mean here?

- Who or what is this about?

- Why did this happen?

- What is the main idea?

- How does this work?

Visualize Strategy

You can **visualize** as you read. Use text details to make pictures in your mind.
- Use the author's words and your own knowledge to help.

- Make mental pictures of people, places, things, actions, and ideas.

PHOTO CREDITS